To Polly
a good friend
who will always be
my good friend —
wherever she goes.

Sharman
June, 1991

SONGS OF THE

FLUTEPLAYER

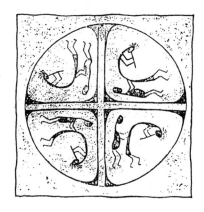

ADDISON-WESLEY

PUBLISHING COMPANY, INC.

READING, MASSACHUSETTS   MENLO PARK, CALIFORNIA

NEW YORK   DON MILLS, ONTARIO   WOKINGHAM, ENGLAN

AMSTERDAM   BONN   SYDNEY   SINGAPORE

TOKYO   MADRID   SAN JUAN   PARIS

SEOUL   MILAN   MEXICO CITY   TAIPEI

SONGS OF THE

FLUTEPLAYER

SEASONS OF LIFE

IN THE SOUTHWEST

SHARMAN APT RUSSELL

Many of the designations used by manufacturers and sellers to distinguish their products are claimed as trademarks. Where those designations appear in this book and Addison-Wesley was aware of a trademark claim, the designations have been printed in initial capital letters (e.g., Coke).

Library of Congress Cataloging-in-Publication Data

Russell, Sharman Apt.
  Songs of the fluteplayer : seasons of life in the Southwest / by Sharman Apt Russell.
        p.   cm.
      ISBN 0-201-57093-9
      1. Farm life—New Mexico—Mimbres River Valley.
2. Mimbres River Valley (N.M.)—Social life and customs.
3. Russell, Sharman Apt. 4. Mimbres River Valley (N.M.)—
Biography.   I. Title.
F802.G7R87   1991
978.9′692′0944—dc20   90-20988
                                                               CIP

Jacket and text design by Linda Koegel
Set in 11-point Garamond No. 3 by Compset, Inc., Beverly, MA.

1 2 3 4 5 6 7 8 9-MW-9594939291
First printing, April 1991

To my mother, Faye Lorrie Apt

CONTENTS

ACKNOWLEDGMENTS

In 1981, newly-wed, my husband and I came to live in a small agricultural valley in southwestern New Mexico. We felt like pioneers. We were on a quest. Most of what has happened since—flood, drought, children, jobs, friendships—has become a part of that first adventure. Like many people, we are constructing our lives out of new and old material, with a mixed sense of wonder and anxiety. When I began writing essays, I began naturally to write the story of that construction, the story of my life here in the Mimbres Valley. Although the incidents in this book are real, the names of neighbors and friends (and in some cases a few personal details) have been changed to protect their privacy. I would like to thank a number of magazines for their support. "The Mimbres" and a version of "Homebirth" first appeared in the *Missouri Review*. "Illegal Aliens" and "Trading Posts" were originally printed in the *Threepenny Review*. "Illegal Aliens" later appeared in *The Pushcart Prize XV* anthology. "Song of the Fluteplayer" was published in *Quarterly West* and "Biosphere II" in the *Massachusetts Review*. This last essay was written with the help of a research grant from Western New Mexico University. I would also like to thank my agent, Felicia Eth, and my editor, Martha Moutray, for their encouragement. Finally, of course, I must thank Peter, my husband.

SONGS OF THE FLUTEPLAYER

THE MIMBRES

Three years before my husband and I bought land on the Mimbres River, an unusual amount of winter snow and spring rain prompted what locals authoritatively called a "hundred-year flood." That left us ninety-seven years. We were also reassured by the large dikes built by the Army Corps of Engineers between our agricultural field and the riverbed. These dense gray mounds of gravel, contained improbably with heavy mesh wire, were ten feet high, twenty-five feet at the base, and ugly. They efficiently blocked our view of the river which, at that time, was not much of a loss. Although things were to change quickly, when we came to southwestern New Mexico, the price of copper stood high, unemployment was low, and—through our land—the Mimbres River stretched bone-dry.

Like many country dwellers not born in the country, we find it hard to believe we were once so naive. We actually sought out river bottom land. We didn't think in terms of rusted wheel bearings, smashed foot bridges, soil erosion, or property damage. We didn't think of rivers at all in terms of property: rivers were above real estate. They were gifts in the desert. They were frail blue lines that disappeared on the map. In the arid Southwest, rivers—even intermittent rivers—were to be coveted.

In the coming years, we came to know the Mimbres River better. On my part, it was not an idyllic relationship. The only road to our house is a rough and rutted trail of packed dirt that goes over the stream bed. When the river does run, about seven months of the year, water seeps into our car bearings and the brakes freeze at night. When the river runs too high, we stall in midstream and must be hauled out by a neighbor's four-wheel drive. Those of us on the wrong side of the Mimbres, a collection of seven families, tried to deal with the conflict of road and river. We got together for workdays and animated discussions in which we all pretended to be engineers. We built an elegant wood and rope "swinging bridge" for pedestrians and at the gravelly bottom of the stream installed cement culverts—only to have both swept away by spring run-off and heavy rains. On the occasion of such rains, the Mimbres became impassable by any vehicle. Whenever this seemed imminent, my husband and I parked our car on the side of the river that led to town: fifty miles to Deming, New Mexico for his teaching job and thirty miles to Silver City for mine. The next day, we would get up painfully early, walk a half mile to the crossing, and wade.

The cold water didn't bother my husband; the problems of this part-time river only intrigued him. In the early 1970s, New Mexico's Soil and Conservation Service had experimented with our section of the Mimbres by cutting down all the cottonwoods. At that time, they believed eliminating these great trees, some more than a hundred years old, would mean more grass for cattle. Today, it seems as inspired an act as putting cans on a cat's tail. Without the cottonwoods to hold the soil with their roots and break the impact of water, subsequent small floods swept over the denuded ground like efficient mowing machines. When the channel was dry again, the eroded result could only charitably be called a river. My husband's dream was to bring the old Mimbres back. To this end, he planted branch after branch of cottonwood in the hope they would miraculously grow. Miraculously, they did. He charted the re-vegetation of willows, chamisa, and walnut. He personally scattered the fluff of cattails. In a meditative silence, he walked the gray dikes built by the Army Corps of Engineers and saw a greener future.

On the morning of the second "hundred-year flood," we woke to a triumphant roar and strangely clear view. Below our house, what had last night been a field of winter rye was a mass of brown water lapping at the goat's pen. Something important seemed to be missing. It took us longer than seems reasonable to realize what that was. The ugly gravel dikes were gone. A strange, dark, churning river had taken their place, a river that also included part of our land, much of our topsoil, and our entire car.

We didn't learn the fate of the Volkswagen until later that morning. Excited and impressed, my husband dressed and went down to inspect the situation. I stayed in the house with our two-month-old daughter. Everyone in the neighborhood was out inspecting, and those who had gotten up early had the chance to see our car—parked on the "town" side of the river—slowly lifted up and carried along in the force of the flood. The little Bug was in good company, with giant cottonwoods torn from their roots and the debris of upstream bridges and irrigation pipe. When my husband returned to confirm the destruction of our single and uninsured vehicle, his face showed a kind of pleasure. Looking out over the changed, aquatic world, his eyes gleamed. He almost laughed. This was a big flood. This was bigger than the last one-hundred-year flood, six years ago. This was a *river*.

Our neighborhood was once a small ranch now divided into forty, ten, and five-acre parcels, with a restriction that no one can further subdivide. This restriction, as well as the property's irrigated land, was part of our reason for being here. We also liked the people who had come before us. As the limited number of house sites sold, a sense of community emerged which resulted in a name: **El Otro Lado** (The Other Side). For our private street sign, Jack and Roberta Greene, among the first to buy, painted this in informal and cock-eyed calligraphy on a wooden board they posted at the highway. Divorced, in his early fifties, Jack had once posted a want ad for a companion in the *Mother Earth News* and thus met the also divorced, forty-eight-year-old Roberta. This slightly comic, slightly suspicious background proved misleading, for the Greenes became our role models, the sanest couple we knew. Neighbors in a rural community, we were all bound by mutual needs. We borrowed hand saws and drill bits from each other's tool box. We shared the maintenance of a Rototiller, and if a friend went out of town, we fed their horses, goats, chickens, dogs, and cats. Inevitably, we were all building passive-solar adobe homes and had much to say to each other about greenhouses and R values. Despite ages that ranged from thirty to sixty, we became close and comfortable and gathered almost every Sunday night—movie night!—around Jack and Roberta's new VCR.

Now, with the flood, we were not alarmed at being cut off and isolated together. Phone lines had been washed away, and the power pole rocked precariously in the middle of the rushing brown water. Huddled in sweaters, we converged as a group to note its sway. Our main fear was that without electricity we could not use the VCR to watch Roberta's copy of a Lina Wertmuller film. The pole held, and a potluck was arranged where, over four different salads, we discussed the river, the weather, and our fields—three words for the same thing.

That easily, the flood became another community event, another movie, another bond.

Upstream, a friend almost lost his life when he tried to cross the water in his new jeep. All night, his pregnant wife walked the crumbling bank and called his name. In the morning he was found clinging to a log, much chastened. His was not the only four-wheeler to go down the river. A small family-owned sawmill contributed some equipment; a rancher lost his prize tractor. The best news, according to everyone, was the loss of the dikes. As it turned out, they had channeled the Mimbres in such a way as to increase its force and power. One landowner threatened to shoot any engineer who tried to re-erect them. This did not prove necessary since the state labeled the entire area a floodplain, a belated nod to nature that prevented further interference.

On our property, the water scoured the river bed as the channel shifted to carve out chunks of irrigated field. When the flood subsided, a matter of days, it left a muddy battleground strewn with logs, misshapen debris, and two rubber tires ten feet in diameter and three feet thick. The small, laboriously planted cottonwoods did not survive. In fact, not a blade of grass remained. Elsewhere on the Mimbres, where the ground had been protected by trees, the torrent overflowed the banks and took down a few of the older cottonwoods. In less than a month, that part of the river was green again.

In southwestern New Mexico, the Mimbres River winds from the pine-covered Gila National Forest, down to the scrub oak and juniper of our land, south to the high plains of the Chihuahuan Desert. In its sixty-mile length, the river drops 4,500 feet and covers four life zones. Narrow, intimate, made lush with irrigation, this area has a long history. I found my first pottery while digging a squash bed in the garden. Since then I have found many bits of clay, their edges irregular, like pieces of a jigsaw puzzle scattered in the dirt. As sometimes happens, the first one was the best: a palm-sized shard of black-on-white ware, its painted lines straight and elegantly thin. Such lines mean that the original pot was made between A.D. 1000 and 1100, the "Classic Period" of the Mimbreno Indians.

In their hundreds of years here, this branch of the Mogollon culture farmed, hunted, gathered, and painted pots that are world-famous today. The designs are often fantastical: southwestern versions of the griffon and the unicorn. Many are natural drawings of animals and insects. Some are quite bawdy—penises as long as your arm! Some resemble Escher paintings with their mirrored images and field reversals. In all, they present an extraordinarily talented culture. Over six thousand Mimbres pots are stored across the world in museums like the Smithsonian; you can also find Mimbres ware for sale, discreetly advertised in the back pages of such magazines as *The New Yorker*. Apparently, once the artistic fervor hit them, these Indians made a lot of pots. Most are found in the burial sites beneath the homes and villages that the Indians abandoned around the thirteenth century. Most have a "kill hole" at the bottom of the bowl, which may have allowed the spirit of the dead to escape. And some scientists theorize that the pots were made exclusively by women, with certain artists or prehistoric celebrities producing on a regular basis.

Modern Mimbrenos are proud of their heritage and exploit it ruthlessly. Designs crafted a thousand years ago can be seen on locally made earrings, T-shirts, stationery, calendars, aprons, towels, and coffee cups. An ancient picture of a bighorn sheep, now extinct in the valley, might pop up on an advertisement for farm equipment or a recruiting poster for the nearby university. While such theft is easily sanctioned, the commercial value of the actual pots is controversial. A Mimbres bowl can be worth as much as $25,000, and pot hunters regularly bulldoze sites that an archeologist might take years to uncover. Pot hunting, of course, is illegal on state or federal land, which most of the valley is not. Although archeologists wax indignant, they are considered by some natives to be just another breed of pot hunters, ones who take their loot to be stored in far-off museums.

In truth, we are all pot hunters here. How could it be otherwise, when the glamor of the past combines with profit? We perk up our ears when we hear that someone down the valley found seventy-two pots in her front yard. Seventy-two! Closer to home—a quarter mile from my doorstep—a doctor and his wife inadvertantly destroyed a Mimbres bowl when dozing a building pad for their new house. On the hill above us, an ancient burial is found complete with human body and turquoise beads.

Such stories confirm that the qualities of a good home site have not changed much in a thousand years. In digging the foundations for our adobe, my husband uncovered a large grinding stone or *metate* buried three feet deep. After that, we watched each shovelful, but no pot emerged that would pay off our land mortgage. Mimbres pots may still be under the forsythia or kitchen floor, but it offends our aesthetics to run about with a backhoe digging arbitrary holes. We remain pleased with the *metate* and, conventionally, keep it outside our doorstep with an associated collection of *manos*: fist-sized, hand-held rocks worn smooth with grinding. Like most people who live in the valley, we count continuum as a return on our money.

Mimbres pottery is glamorous for its age and beauty. But it is only part of a small museum scattered over our twelve acres. A band of Apaches called the *Tci-he-nde* or Red Paint people left their arrowheads, as well as a four-inch spearpoint now on a shelf of knickknacks. Named for a stripe of paint across the warrior's face, this tribe probably entered the area long after the Mimbrenos' exit. They continued the tradition of farming. At least, they tended their crops between times on the warpath, first with the Spanish and later with the Mexicans and Americans. In the nineteenth century, chiefs like Mangas Coloradas and Victorio found it increasingly hard to hold off the growing horde of gold-hungry, silver-hungry, copper-hungry, even meershaum-hungry miners. Where miners went, forts and soldiers followed. And by the late 1860s, Mexican and Anglo farmers had also settled the Mimbres and would supply the boom town of Silver City with bumper crops of potatoes. Such early entrepreneurs dry-farmed pinto beans where my front yard yields grama grass. In 1869, they established the irrigation system that waters my garden. Over the years, these men and women dropped their own mementos of baling wire, lavender glass, and bone white china. Most recently, I found in our field a perfect 6 1/2 ounce Coke bottle. Its thick shape, patterned with raised letters, dated from the 1940s—seemingly an emblem of the modern world, until we compared the heavy diminutive bottle with an aluminum can red-flagged NutraSweet.

The Mimbrenos, the Apaches, the dry farmers are all gone—and not just because they died. The sudden disappearance of the Mimbrenos, along with Indian groups like the Anasazi to the north, is still a mystery. In their ruins is a sense of calm which seems to preclude war or pestilence. Their dead are properly buried, their kitchen utensils neatly stored. In contrast, the Apaches were clearly driven out. At one point, an Indian agent promised them a reservation on their homeland, but the citizens of Silver City objected, and nothing came of it. In 1886, the famed year that Geronimo surrendered, the entire Red Paint people were put on boxcars and shipped to Florida and permanent exile. For the dry farmers, the weather simply changed, and it began to rain less. The river itself was no longer that "rapid, dashing stream, about fifteen feet wide and three feet deep" described in 1846 by an American soldier.

Oddly, or perhaps not, such disappearances continue today. They are a part of the valley's heritage. In the ten years we have lived here, we have seen most of our friends and many of our acquaintances leave. Most obviously, a failing local economy is to blame. The Mimbres Valley is in Grant County, one of New Mexico's richest mineralized areas. Twelve miles to the east, the Santa Rita Mines began producing copper as early as 1804, and for most of the twentieth century that yellow metal—not quite so yellow as gold but more abundant—was excavated from a hole that eventually swallowed the entire town of Santa Rita, including its hospital and schoolhouse. Mining is an extractive industry. In the 1980s, the Kennicott Mining Company declared that only forty years worth of low-grade ore existed at the strip mine they advertised as "the world's prettiest copper pit." Many smaller operations in nearby Hanover and Pinos Altos had already played out, and the other major company in the area, Phelps Dodge, also began to count the years. No one employed by the mines paid much attention. No one even mentioned it to newcomers like us, and we didn't ask. As it turned out, forty was not the magic and seemingly far-off number. For it wasn't the amount of copper that caught Grant County by surprise, but the price per pound. By the time that price fell to under fifty-eight cents in 1982, the layoffs had already begun.

Still, that is only part of the story. Most of our friends did not leave the Mimbres Valley because they could not find a job here but because they could not find the job they expected of life. They and we came to this area for the small-town ambiance and rural lifestyle. Not surprisingly, neither the small town nor the surrounding rural area required many editors, landscape architects, graphic designers, psychologists, or political lobbyists. More surprisingly, some of us discovered that we needed to be these things. We had embraced a concept of happiness that required escape from the contaminated, stressful cities. For love of land—for love of beauty, for love of the valley—we could adjust to a lower standard of living. We could not adjust (at least not all of us) to being high school teachers or car mechanics.

Our closest neighbor is the car mechanic. His real interest is solar energy systems, and he wonders why his back hurts and why he spends his time under the hoods of cars as old as himself. Another friend would like to build houses but the economy here is too depressed and he lives, instead, on odd carpentry jobs. For five years, my husband was the high school teacher. Because of the long drive, he left for work at six in the morning and returned from work when it was too dark to see the land he was working to pay for. Increasingly, he became frustrated by conditions in his job which prevented him from doing it well. He was angered by the blatent cultural contempt for teachers, even as he recognized in himself echos of that contempt. As one close relative told him, public school teaching is a "deviant career choice." Even the school administrators seemed to agree. Finally, for a number of reasons, none of which had to do with low salary or discipline problems, my husband left Deming High.

It hardly needs to be said that he does not want to leave the Mimbres Valley. For now he pursues part-time work which includes free-lance photography and outfitting in the Gila Wilderness. Together with my salary, this income does not add up to what we have discovered—another surprise—we would like to have. Still, in the privacy of the valley, we can pick and choose our conveniences. We have an outhouse; we also have a word processor. Social identity, not economics, is perhaps the more real dilemma. What is a man with a patchwork of jobs as insecure as our river? Will my husband be happy at the age of fifty-five?

We don't know the answers to these questions, and in the willful charting of our lives, we wonder what turns we are taking and what roads we irrevocably pass. We wonder if we will ever regret our choice to step outside what we were taught to consider the mainstream. Perhaps we should wonder why we feel that it was a choice, as though how and why we came here was a conscious navigation, as though we are not, all of us, riding logs down a river.

In the theme of departure, there are variations. Jack and Roberta Greene retired here to build a home, garden, and become potters. Together, that first year, they made enough forty-pound adobe bricks for a small, liveable studio. They would need another two thousand for their one-bedroom house. Meanwhile they planted an orchard of peaches, plums, apples, cherries, and walnuts. A master gardener, Roberta also grew lavish rows of strawberries, chilies, tomatoes, lettuce, peas, eggplant, cucumbers, onions, leeks, radishes, potatoes, and corn. Their raspberry crops were famous. It was far more food than they could eat, and in the summer they took the surplus to Silver City's Farmer's Market. In their second year, the two thousand adobe bricks lay neatly stacked in lines that spilled over into Jack's vinyard. Enthusiastically, they began to lay up the walls. Jack studied wiring, and they did most of the work themselves, including a compost toilet and solar hot-water system. By the time they had been in the valley five years, they had a beautiful Santa Fe-style home, an established orchard, a shed of useful tools, and the acceptable identity of a retired couple. As part of the grand plan, Jack began a kiln for their pottery work.

We profited greatly from the Greenes' knowledge, as well as from their tool shed. But by the time we began to lay up our own walls, Jack and Roberta were showing signs of restlessness. Before his "radicalization" and divorce, Jack had owned a chain of liquor stores in California. Twenty years later, with a beard and a wife from *Mother Earth News,* he was still the businessman, still a driver. The dream house was built. Now he couldn't quite see truck gardening for minimum wage or making pots for less than that. One day he and Roberta bought a video store in Silver City. At that time, it was the only video store in town and contained less than fifty movies. With Jack's retailing expertise and the labor Roberta once spent on her garden, the business grew quickly. For a while, the Greenes tried to straddle two worlds.

But inevitably the "simple life" (burning and hauling trash, commuting to town, crossing the river, chasing cows from the garden, fixing a broken windmill, canning tomatoes) proved too burdensome. Some time after the second hundred-year flood, they bought a furnished house in town and put the Mimbres adobe up for sale.

In the nineteenth century, the French visitor Alexis de Tocqueville observed "An American will build a house in which to pass his old age and sell it before the roof is on; he will plant a garden and rent it just as the trees are bearing; he will clear a field and leave others to reap the harvest; he will take up a profession and leave it, settle in one place and soon go off elsewhere with his changing desires."

My husband used to quote this in wonderment. Now we see how easily it could apply to us. When Jack and Roberta left, taking with them our Sunday night movies, the disintegration of our community began. The car mechanic opened up a bicycle shop in Silver City, and it is only a matter of time before he moves there too. The wife of one couple is in law school in Albuquerque. Another neighbor job hunts in Santa Fe. As we count the number of friends who have left the valley, as well as El Otro Lado, we are surprised at their number. Suddenly, we are no longer newcomers; we are the ones who are left.

On the river bank, my husband has planted more cottonwoods. With the dikes gone, he hopes this batch will survive the next flood. Many cottonwoods have already started up on their own, for this, after all, is the work of flooding—to tear down dying trees and carry seeds to new parts of the river. The chamisa is returning too and small patches of willow. Although it has only been a few years, the flood seems to have happened long ago, to much younger people. These days, my husband broods over the increase of mobile homes in the valley: the tiny aluminum squares that mar his view of rolling hills and the fang of Cooke's Peak. Insistent against a backdrop of mesas, these trailers represent a different vision of the country, a vision we had not foreseen as overnight they pop up on the treeless tracts of land a son is carving from his father's pasture. The valley, like the river, can not be predicted.

In the marital urge for balance, we switch sides often now. This week it is I who grow depressed at the thought of leaving the Mimbres Valley. It is not only the green fields that hold me, but the loss of my naivete. I am not sure I want to spend another ten years learning new lessons. Here, at least, we know our enemies. In this mood, I tell my husband that mobile homes are democratic. I tell him that new friends will come. I tell him that he will find the right job or find he doesn't need to. I tell him that the next flood will be a hundred years away and, in the meantime, his cottonwoods will grow tall. Let's stay, I say this week. Let's stay.

ILLEGAL ALIENS

Every year, for the past many years, over a million illegal aliens are arrested as they cross the sometimes invisible line that defines and encloses the United States of America. In the El Paso sector—a pastel-colored desert stretching from Van Horn, Texas to the western end of New Mexico—hundreds of thousands of "undocumented men and women" are caught annually by the Border Patrol, with an estimated twice that number passing through undeterred. A small percentage of this traffic will come through the Mexican town of Palomas, which in English means dove and which lies a mile south of Columbus, New Mexico and its desultory border checkpoint. Most Mexicans crossing through Palomas are seasonal workers who expect to return via the same route. Over the years, what has come to pass for industry in Palomas is a strip of adobe storefronts, brothels, and hotels used by such men coming home with their new-won wages shoved deep in pockets or sewn into the hems of clothing. From nearby ranching and mining communities, Anglos have helped build up this trade in sex and recreation. Although Mexicans entering the States are not likely to partake of the town's luxuries, this is not to say they don't plan to on their return.

From Palomas, an even smaller percentage of *mojados* or "wet ones" will choose to walk up through the sparse creosote of the Chihuahuan Desert, past the town of Deming on Interstate 10, past—walking steadily on, in their fifth day by now—the thrust of Cooke's Peak with its barrel cactus and hidden shelves of pictographs. Under the shadow of this mountain, these men will gravitate to the green-lined Mimbres River and follow its cottonwoods up a narrow valley of irrigated fields and apple orchards. Here, sometimes alone, sometimes in groups of two or three, they might begin to look for work. By the time they reach my house, at the northern end of the valley, the memory of Palomas belongs to another life, another country, and they will have walked nearly a hundred miles.

When I first came to the Mimbres, I often saw illegal aliens traveling purposefully at the edge of the road and my peripheral vision. I did not recognize them as such, although in defineable and undefineable ways they seemed out of place on the black-topped highway. As I drove, silver mailboxes flashed by with the inevitable dirt road, adobe home, or trailer attached. Cattle and horses grazed on the brown hills of grama grass. Fields blazed green along the banks of the river. Against this setting, there was something odd about the isolation of these men dressed in polyester pants and carrying a paper sack, small bag, or bundle of clothing. Miles from any town, they did not hitchhike and did not seem to be walking to or from a car. Strangely detached, they kept their gaze directed ahead, on a focus which resolved not on the road but at someone's door. The door opened, and the man or woman inside had something for them to do: adobes to make, walls to lay up, fences to fix, or—less satisfactorily—a garden to weed.

In my late twenties and by all standards an adult, I had never thought of myself as an employer, much less one who hired people who hid when a police car passed. So when the men began to appear at my door with their diffident smiles and gestures, I felt uneasy. I did not know how to respond to their questions, how to supply food or even water. Not speaking Spanish was my excuse. But the truth lay more in the way they looked. They looked different. They looked poor. And they were, after all, men. I imagine that in the 1930s other women shared my feelings when the hobos first began to appear on porch steps. Like these women, I adapted, in surprisingly little time, to the stranger at the door.

As the crow flies, the Mimbres Valley lies over a hundred miles north of the nearest metropolis (El Paso), thirty miles east of the nearest town (population 12,000), and directly south of the Gila National Forest. It is hard to make a living here and we miss the proximity of bookstores and corner cafes. In this rural area, our neighbors divide neatly into those who live here because it is familiar and those who came here because it is not. Most of my friends fall in the latter category, and for us the subject of illegal aliens was new and interesting. One friend, who speaks French and Spanish and who has tried unsuccessfully to serve his workers **borsht,** described the knock at the door as an "informal cultural exchange program." He wrote down the addresses of men he liked and assumed that one day he would visit and be welcomed. Another friend argued that hiring aliens takes jobs from Americans who would work for less if the welfare system were suitably altered. To this, a third friend responded that Mexicans need to work as much as anyone and that she hires for humanness, not nationality.

Some of us theorized that the flow of unemployed and ambitious out of Mexico gave that country a necessary release valve and prevented turmoil, i.e., revolution. This idea, too, divided into two camps: those who thought it was good to prevent revolution and those who thought it was not. From a different viewpoint, many of us believed the current system—in which "aliens" were illegal but hiring an alien was not—wrong because it permitted too much abuse. We all knew of the rancher who turned his workers into the Immigration Service the day before payday. Other employers withheld pay until the job was completed and, in the meantime, fed their workers poorly. It was easy to see how inequity could flourish when the employed had no avenue of complaint or redress. At the same time, we also all knew scores of perfectly decent people—a Hispanic farmer in Deming or a chili grower in Hatch—whose small business depended on alien labor.

More to the point was the Mexican couple who had dinner with us one winter night, a week before Christmas. She was eight months pregnant. He was desperately seeking work. We told them that with the layoffs at the copper mine, unemployment in our county had reached 40 percent. He replied it was 80 percent where he came from. They had just walked nine days in the cold and rain. We did not suggest they turn around and go back.

Increasingly, it seemed that the problem of undocumented men and women could only be examined one focal length at a time. There was the big picture, and there was a man with a bundle of clothes. As one came into focus, the other blurred.

In any event, for my husband and me, the discussions were academic. We learned to give food. We pointed directions. We sometimes chatted. But when asked about work, we spoke without thinking, without hesitation. *"No trabajo."* No work here.

Then we began to build.

In southwestern New Mexico, building an adobe home is an intense rite of passage which requires, in its purest form, no previous construction experience. For financial reasons, we started with one large room. After the kind of research that involves a lot of driving and staring at other people's houses, we decided to make a traditional mountain adobe altered by passive-solar, south-facing windows. As teachers, we had the summer to make the bricks, lay up the walls, and put on the sloping hipped tin roof. This was traditional "wetback" work, but we never gave a thought to hiring someone else. We would do it together, alone.

It began well. Although a good adobero can talk at interminable length about R values and thermal efficiency, he or she knows that transformation is the truer miracle. A patch of soil becomes a bedroom. Solid ground is transmogrified into a windowsill. An unsightly hole will be a wall nine feet high. For us, such miracles depended upon a borrowed and ancient cement mixer whose idiosyncrasies were my bane as I shoveled dirt and sprayed water into its maw. The mud was then wheelbarrowed away by my husband and poured into a wooden form for three bricks fourteen-by-ten-by-four inches.

Adobe is a cunning mixture of clay and sand. Too much clay and the brick cracks while drying, too little and it lacks strength. We tested the proportions of our soil by throwing handfuls of dirt into a jar of water, shaking vigorously, and watching the layers settle. Amazingly, our land appeared to be a huge dehydrated adobe mix—add water, stir, and pour. This we did, every day, ten hours a day, for three weeks. It was hard work, but not unpleasant. Transformation! The ground formed into squares that we set on their sides to dry and then gingerly stacked. On one good day, eighty wet-looking bricks lay in soldierly rows before us. On most days, there were only sixty or fifty. We ended up with thirteen hundred adobes: a hundred less than we thought we should have, a hundred more than we would actually need.

While we waited two weeks for the bricks to dry, we began to dig the foundation footings, which had to be large to support the heavy walls. In a matter of days, etched deep in the ground, our room became defined. Into these holes, we inserted stakes of metal to which we fastened, at a ninety-degree angle, the longer slim poles of steel rebar. There was something elegant about these complex layers, running in their rectangle of fifteen-by-twenty feet. I almost hated to cover them with cement. I hated it even more as we began to do it, for cement is nothing at all like adobe. The magic was gone, or rather, reversed. It had become bad magic. At the mixer, I glumly shoveled in heavy gravel and two buckets of cement. Moistened with water, the backbreaking load was then dumped into the wheelbarrow which my husband manfully directed in tottering form to the foundation's edge. The stuff slopped out to disappear into the earth. Again, the process was repeated and another load swallowed. Again, another load, and another, as our muscles strained and our skin split from the alkaline lime.

At this point, things went downhill. There is a Mimbres Valley saying that the couple who builds together divorces together. As our visions of the house altered, diverged, and then collided, as our bodies reminded us that that we were only getting older, we moved from bad temper to the kind of free-floating anger rooted in childhood. Through a haze of misunderstandings, we peeled pine logs for *vigas,* built forms for the next step of the foundation, and eternally mixed more cement. At night, we talked about the house rather than sensibly talking about other things. One day, I left for a brief respite in town. On another day, so did my husband.

When the dust settled, we began again.

Down the road, our neighbor has a small trailer where he once housed illegal Mexican workers who came every year and built what seemed to us a dizzying array of fences. That summer, two young men were busy digging holes on his land, erecting posts, and nailing up expensive-looking wire. They began each day at eight and when they stopped at five the afternoon stretched before them, light and long and empty of things to do. One evening, in the cooling hours of midsummer, they wandered over to watch us lay our sixth course of adobe. With finicky slowness we placed each brick flush to the outside string that served as our level. At intervals, we also put wooden blocks where we estimated heavy pictures or cupboards would go. At that time we agreed, quite incorrectly, that it would be easy enough to install the electrical wires later.

My husband, who speaks Spanish, offered our visitors a beer and conversation. He inquired as to what part of Mexico they came from. Chihuahua? A nice city. He had been there. He wanted to know the latest exchange rate for pesos. He asked how many adobes they could make in a day. Four hundred? We looked at each other. He asked the Spanish word for hammer. He told them he was a high school teacher.

At five the next afternoon, they showed up again. This time, they clamored into the room like a crew just hired. One took over my task of lifting up the forty-pound brick; another elbowed my husband aside and demonstrated the proper way of setting the adobe in its mortar of mud. They stayed until the sun tipped over the ridge of our western hills. They had taken pity on us.

Although we offered, neither Manuel nor Gabriel wanted money. They liked the cold slide of our beer at the end of the day. But more, they liked the companionship of working with equals. This was their free time, their gift. For two more weeks, they came uncalled when their own day was through—and we, who also had been working since eight and who would work on until dark, were in their debt. The relationship between American and "wetback" turned on its head, and some tension in us relaxed. That next summer, when we started building again, we understood well that we had plenty of work for a skilled adobero. So we began our career of hiring illegal aliens.

Effrem and Jesus sat rather stiffly on the edge of the couch while Shirley Grijalva—rodeo rider and mother of three—spoke swiftly to them in Spanish and then as swiftly to us in English. Shirley knew Effrem well; he was an "old friend" and we were letting her handle the negotiations with our first employees. At that time, in 1983, the going rate was eight dollars a day, plus food and board. (In the next four years, the price would rise to ten or twelve dollars, with strenuous work on a farm or ranch paying fifteen and more. At that time, most wage earners in Mexico were getting the equivalent of three dollars a day.) We offered a dollar above the norm and consulted with Shirley as to what was board. Beans, she said. Beans, meat, tortillas, eggs, potatoes, coffee, and canned food. Effrem, she noted, preferred white bread to tortillas. Employers also had the option of providing cigarettes, beer, and the occasional pair of socks. We would do that, we agreed quickly. We believed in keeping Mexican wages, nine dollars a day, intact for the trip home to Mexico.

I was never to know Effrem or Jesus very well or, for that matter, any of the men who eventually worked for us. Each morning, my husband and they conferred, gathered tools, and went off together making more adobes, stuccoing walls, or digging ditches. I went inside our now completed room to my own projects and, later, child-rearing duties. At lunchtime I cooked a hot meal of beans, eggs, and tortillas which the three men ate outside in the shade of the patio. Then I washed the dishes. In the late afternoon, I prepared a bag of dinner and breakfast food for the workers to take and cook in our neighbor's trailer. My husband

and I assumed these segregated roles because we believed that the men would be more comfortable if we did so. Certainly, I felt a need to appear "traditional" and did not, for example, publicly contradict my husband's building ideas (something I did in private) or wear short skirts while hanging up the laundry. My job, as I saw it, was to oil these days, in which we were getting a great deal of work done, with a flow of domesticity.

What I learned, I learned in the evening, second hand. Effrem, my husband told me, had six children and four hundred acres in Chihuahua. Most of his land was scrub desert. The rest was a small but viable apple orchard. Early in the summer, before his harvest, he fell short of cash and came up to the States. In his late forties, his dark hair touched by gray, Effrem proved to be slow, reliable, and meticulous in his work. His gentle manners and soft voice made him seem a very serious man, a family man, sensitive and thoughtful.

Jesus provided a contrast. While Effrem looked broad and solid, Jesus had a tall skinny frame that alternated between nervous energy and an indolent loll. With the dapper moustache and groomed hair appropriate to a twenty-two-year-old, Jesus was full of plans, the owner of a future in which the strokes were broad and the details still vague. Already, he boasted, he had traveled as far south as Nicaragua and as far north as Washington. He was out to see the world, on a young man's lark that required financing along the way. More voluble than Effrem, Jesus came up with a running series of deals. Would we contract to lay the tiles instead of paying a daily wage? Would we sell his cousin in

El Paso our old car? Would we hire another worker, a good friend of his, who could do the finish work we so clearly needed? When it came time for Jesus to go, he asked us for a pair of Converse tennis shoes. No matter the cost, he said with largesse, he would pay. We shopped around and came up with a better price, not a Converse, but a good shoe. No, Jesus said. The brand name was important.

Effrem and Jesus promised to return the next summer. Effrem did and first went to work for one of our neighbors, whom he didn't much like. After a week he moved on and settled further north as a ranch hand. From another young man who stopped at our house, we were shocked to learn that Jesus had been shot to death in a Palomas bar. The young man added that Jesus had been a *coyote,* a descriptive term for those who take money from aliens—usually refugees fleeing Central America—in exchange for transporting them across the border.

The same grapevine that spread the news of Jesus's death also put us on the circuit as a place to stop for information, food, and a day or two of work. By now, we knew that although we could hire aliens and transport them in a southerly direction, there were serious penalties for driving an alien north: possible fines, imprisonment, and an impounded car. We knew that, on their way home, some men liked to be picked up by the green trucks bearing the Immigration's seal—*la Migra,* as we called them. Depending on where they lived, this could save them a walk and usually meant they wound up in an American cell overnight where their money might be safer than on the road. On the other hand, it could also mean being turned over for a shakedown to the Mexican authorities. For this reason, some workers liked their pay put in a postal order they could send home. Others didn't.

That was the summer Ernesto and his "son Luis" came to help us put on an adobe floor for our second room. Ernesto would continue to help us at various tasks for the next three years. He was a small man, possibly in his sixties, with gray stubble and ropy muscles. Each season he came accompanied by a male relative whom he always referred to as his son Luis. Sometimes it was his son. As likely, it could have been a grandson, cousin, or son-in-law. Once the man's name was actually Luis. For the others, their real names only emerged gradually in conversation. This simplification of relationships and names was, I think, Ernesto's version of making the Anglos comfortable.

Ernesto's forte was stonework, and although we didn't plan on terracing our back yard with dry stone walls, his expertise convinced us. Like Effrem, he worked slowly and steadily. The younger relative played the role of helper, fetching the stones in a wheelbarrow and lounging, bored, while Ernesto made his selections. If necessary, Ernesto would trim the stone with a sharp blow of his hammer before fitting it carefully into its arranged niche. The result was a layered work of art, which Ernesto would always want to cap with cement—a practical touch we always vetoed.

In our longer relationship with Ernesto, we learned more about familial patterns and life in Mexico. We watched the pecking order quickly established between relatives, the respect given Ernesto as a skilled worker, and the way in which he jealously guarded his skills. No hands but his placed the stone, for he did not jeopardize his livelihood by teaching it—at least, not yet. We knew that by extending our house into three rooms, 1,000 square feet, we were doubling the size of Ernesto's home. By the fourth year, too, we had worked twice with the son-in-law whose name was really Luis. A genial but restless man with five children, he was widowed when we first met him and newly married the second summer. His first wife, Ernesto's daughter, had died in childbirth and the son-in-law was still coming to the States to pay off the doctor's bill. "I was a screwball for marrying again," he said in Spanish to my husband, and Ernesto agreed.

Because of our growing sense of familiarity, even friendship, it remained a shock when the morning came that we did not see Ernesto and his relative walking up the hill to our house. By nine o'clock we knew they were not coming, and we realized that once again they had left suddenly without telling us. We understood now, but did not condone, why some employers paid at the end of the job. It was to ensure that the job get done, that the adobe bricks were not left unfinished in the rain or a wall half-stuccoed or a floor half-laid. Here, at least, unreliability was the alien's trademark and privilege. His abrupt departures illustrated how tenuous the relationship really was and how unbound by social rules. Sometimes the explanation got back to us: a brother had fallen ill or a child was born. Sometimes the men left because they had an argument in the trailer, or because they were tired of working, or because they were homesick. Since Ernesto didn't trust the postal system, he would be carrying all his money in a handkerchief wadded tightly in his pocket. If he had worked as long as two weeks, that would be $120 in savings—equal in Mexico to two months work. If he was lucky, Ernesto would avoid *La Migra*'s green trucks. If he was lucky, he would catch a ride on the highway and spend the night, not on the road, but in a Palomas hotel.

In June of 1988 a new immigration law began to impose penalties on the employers of illegal aliens. The law requires any employer to ask for documentation—a birth certificate, passport, or driver's license—before hiring. If the employer does not and hires an illegal alien, he or she is liable to a civil fine ranging from $250 to $2,000. For a second offense, the penalty can rise to $5,000 per worker. A third offense may mean six months in jail. (There are, however, many exceptions and workers in certain crops are exempt.) The law also provided amnesty and American citizenship for aliens who had been living in the country since January 1982. Amnesty, of course, did not affect the men we knew since they did not want American citizenship; they wanted to work here seasonally and return to their own country. How the act did affect them is unclear. In some parts of the country, studies seem to show that the 1988 Immigration Law has not significantly stopped the flow of illegal workers. But here in the Mimbres Valley, Ernesto and his relatives do not come anymore. I rarely see men like them along the edge of the highway. And no one drops by our house to ask for food or work.

In truth, we could not say that we would hire any alien who did come. Now that we too risk being illegal, we would have to think that through all over again. We never really knew what we were doing. We never found an answer, right or wrong, but in the end responded to personal needs, ours and theirs. We let the big picture blur and focused on the small. It seemed to work for a time.

SONG OF THE FLUTEPLAYER

I n that interior world, that landscape which is another home, two men live inside me. One, not really a man, is Kokopelli, a prehistoric hunchbacked fluteplayer drawn on pottery and scratched in rock walls throughout northern Mexico and the American Southwest. The other figure, closer to my heart, is a test pilot—my father—who crashed in the Mohave desert in 1956. As they walk bare-boned hills and clamor up banks of sand to new vistas, I doubt that these two ever meet. More truthfully, there is much about them I do not know.

When I first saw Kokopelli, I didn't like him. On a cold gray day for which we had underdressed, my husband and I had just walked an hour to reach Commanche Cave in Hueco Tanks Historical Park, east of El Paso, Texas. The word cave proved an exaggeration for this hole in a cactus-studded cliff of crumbling rock. Dark and smelling of urine, the overhanging ledge might have held ten people if they huddled closely together. Its title was another misnomer since the drawings here are from the Mescalero Apache, a Plains people forced out of their hunting grounds by the Commanche. On that Saturday afternoon, a group of male teen-agers had arrived before us and were sniggering loudly, already drunk as they eyed the painted figure of a humpbacked man whose erection stretched out larger than his head and as long as his legs. About to penetrate the vagina of a standing woman, Kokopelli's penis eerily duplicated the shape of a nearby, giant snake. Defacing the snake was the name Candaleria spray-painted in black. Although the Apaches viewed this cave as sacred—the abode of supernatural beings—in this ambiance, the well-endowed fluteplayer simply looked lustful and arrogant, grafitti from the past with a simple enough message. My own response was tinged with prudery. Alcohol, sex, snakes: I was not in the mood.

Some time later, in my second encounter with Kokopelli, I was alone and the fluteplayer came upon me suddenly, unsought and unplanned. Surrounded only by rock and sky and desert, the glimpse of a petroglyph can be like the sighting of a wild and possibly dangerous animal. It can stop your breath. Daringly I touched the etched figure, which was large, perhaps two feet high, while in the canyon behind me wind whistled through scrub oak and smoothed the fractured surface of pink stone. For a moment I felt the keen clutch of greed: this was the closest I would ever come to finding buried treasure. At the same time I had the requisite emotion of awe. The valley where I live was once populated by the Mimbreno Indians, and this particular fluteplayer could well be a thousand years old, an age that hovered outside my range of belief. Here, drawn on a flat rock twenty miles from my home, the fluteplayer was caught in one of his many transformations into a bug or odd-shaped creature. Already his hump had formed the curved shell of a locust and his antenna streamed behind him as his arms shortened into an insect's legs. Here, as in Commanche Cave, he had the power to repel and slightly frighten. He had the reek of that which is half-human and half-beast, a cunning, scrabbling magic that, like a man with a giant penis, was alien to me.

Since then I have seen other Kokopellis, many of them, tootling under a high ledge at Canyon de Chelly or dancing among the ruins of Chaco Canyon. The humpbacked fluteplayer first began to appear around A.D. 700 and today is the single most recognizable figure from southwestern prehistory. In Colorado, he shoots mountain sheep with a bow and arrow. In central New Mexico, he wields his instrument like a club against a huge, long-clawed grizzly. In some drawings he wears a headdress of rabbity ears and appears to represent the game itself. In other petroglyphs, scattered among the buttes of Arizona and Utah, he reclines gracefully, his flute pointed to the sky and his legs kicking up with the self-absorption of a baby. Most often, the musician is related to sexual prowess: he is a gregarious Don Juan and fertility symbol. In my favorite Mimbres bowl, he has the dapper look of an uninhibited Fred Astaire, with twinkly lines that radiate from his eyes and a phallus he holds lovingly in one hand.

At some point in the thirteenth century, the prehistoric cultures—from the Mimbrenos to the Anasazi and the desert Hohokam—disappeared, fragmented, and spun across the Southwest to re-emerge as the Pueblo, Papago, and Pima Indians. Kokopelli followed. In Hopi legends he is the fluteplaying Locust:

a Promethean figure who submits to painful tests so that man-
kind can live on earth. The Zunis call him a rain priest with the
power to bring down clouds. In Papago myths, he carries the
seeds of spring in his ever-useful hump, which has been known
to hold babies, corn, and buckskin for making moccasins. Late-
comers to the Southwest also incorporated the fluteplayer into
their storytelling. The Navajos call him Watersprinkler. The
Apache drew him in their sacred caves.

The disguises of Kokopelli intrigue me. At the Hopi village
of Hano on First Mesa, he is a black man, probably a version of
the Spanish Moor Esteban who, in 1539, guided Fray Marcos de
Niza north to discover the Seven Cities of Gold. This tale is as
weird and flamboyant as the conquistadors themselves, as flamboyant as the slave Esteban who chose to go ahead of the monk
and represent himself as a god. Accompanied by two greyhounds,
Esteban adorned his arms and legs with feathers and bells, shook
painted gourds, and demanded turquoise and women as tribute.
At a Zuni pueblo, the Indians called his bluff. A god, they reasoned, would be able to prevent himself from being killed and
cut into tiny pieces. Horrified, Fray Marcos de Niza returned to
Mexico to set Coronado in motion, while certain Tewa Indians,
guests at the pueblo, carried on the gossip of a dark-skinned ras-
cal, recast today in a black humped katchina doll named Kokopelli.

In other Hopi villages, the fluteplayer is also a katchina or
divine spirit who appears as a seducer of naive girls. In one story,
Kokopelli hides in a hole in the ground near where a beautiful
maiden relieves herself. Using a hollow tube fashioned from

reeds, he directs his extraordinarily flexible organ up into the unsuspecting girl. "Hardly had she finished than she felt something stirring under her," goes the tale, "and enjoying the sensation, made no effort to investigate." After that, "Kokopelli never failed to take advantage of his device nor did the girl abandon her customary visits to this spot." Eventually, the "virgin" had a child and the fluteplayer managed to prove his fatherhood and win himself a bride.

I like such stories, for what I first feared in Kokopelli—hungry, lewd, billygoat sex—I now find admirable. Perhaps it is only that I have grown more used to his ways. Or perhaps I have grown up more myself. I envy his passion now. I have seen enough of his dancing to know there is no arrogance in it.

For archeologists, the fluteplayer's range in time and space gives him a rare solidity. Naturally such a figure attracts speculation. Who was Kokopelli really? Where did he come from? What does he mean?

In 1936, a physician and amateur archeologist named Dr. Gerald B. Webb declared that the curved spine and misshapen hump of the fluteplayer was proof of tuberculosis in prehistoric America. "It is of special interest," wrote the doctor, "that in the pictographs the artists have indicated paralysis of the legs. The individuals are on their backs, and playing the flute, a suggestion of occupational therapy!"

Obviously, Dr. Webb was unaware of Kokopelli's range of interests. But his theory was accepted as fact until 1960, when another researcher looked more closely at the evidence of skeletal remains. A later report in the *Journal of the American Medical As-*

sociation found Kokopelli the victim of misdiagnosis and sent him on his way.

By this time, another theory was making the rounds. Most archeologists agree that Kokopelli "diffused upward" from the south to northern Mexico and the American Southwest. In this spread of culture, a main source of influence was the *pochteca* or trader: a solitary merchant who traveled up and down the continent exchanging goods such as macaws, shells, pyrite mirrors, peyote, slaves, and turquoise. In the *pochteca* theory, the hump on Kokopelli's back is actually a pack of goods, and one botanist has suggested that the Quichua Indians of the Andes are the specific ancestors of Kokopelli. Evidence of this lies in plant genetics. Ancient ears of a pod corn found in Arizona ruins are similar to a relic corn commonly stocked by Bolivian medicine men; in the mid-twentieth century, these merchants were still traveling through South and Central America playing their traditional reed flute, carrying a small blanket-pack, and selling the corn as a cure for respiratory problems. In this version, Kokopelli becomes the original traveling salesman, a role he fits rather well.

For myself, the *pochteca* theory is especially appealing, for it allows me to imagine a human being, alone but for his wits, in the vastness of a wild unknown. Brought up on tales of the Western frontier, I transform the trader into the explorer, and I can feel the excitement, the glamour, the singing that runs through the veins: *Over this hill! Look! I shall call it the Grand Canyon. Mother of God! A beast with a ringed tail!*

Anyone who has ever gone on a walk will recognize the phenomena. It is the pull of around the bend. It is the urge to quest, to prowl like an animal, to discover like a human being. The mythology of the western hemisphere is wondrous not because it is a story of progression—the Bronze Age followed by more metals still—but because it reveals a pristine and relatively uninhabited land. A few Mimbrenos here, a Hohokam village there. But mostly land. Huge, undulating, full of surprises.

None of this has much to do with the *pochteca* of early Mesoamerica, whose experiences likely revolved around homesickness and an early death. Nor has it much to do with the reality of my life. I have tried to camp alone in the woods and desert, and I usually find myself bored and lonely. I read ethnobotany with voyeuristic pleasure; I cherish the thought of stripping mesquite beans into a yucca basket or of grinding acorns into meal. But I am also an unredeemed lover of junk food. I do not even like to cook and feel sure I would resent the hours needed to dig up, prepare, and bake an agave root.

No, we are talking metaphor here. We are being symbolic. We are in that interior world.

In that world, in my own theory of Kokopelli, the fluteplayer is the man, the woman, compelled to wander through beauty and danger. He is sexy, naturally, for in a more natural and unclothed world, who could deny the power of sex? He is merry because he is in contact with something wonderful in the land. He is also imperfect and vulnerable. He carries a hump. He requires a flute for his music. He is Ulysses, Don Quixote, and Amelia Earhart. He is the loner, the cowboy, the self-sufficient, archetypal, numinous hero.

This brings me to my father, who was also a hero as our culture and the dictionary define one. Born in 1924, my father grew up during the Depression milking cows and plucking chickens on the family farm in eastern Kansas. At seventeen, when stories of the "European War" filled the newspapers, he joined the Air Corps and served as a fighter pilot in the Caribbean. When World War II ended, he went on to graduate as an aeronautical engineer from a midwestern university. Eventually he ended up at the experimental test pilot training program at Edwards Air Force Base in California—the mecca of military aviation research in the 1950s, the home of the Air Research and Development Command, and of its handmaiden the Air Force Flight Test Center.

On the edge of the Mohave Desert, Edwards Air Force Base is a thin layer of steel and concrete laid over a brown landscape dotted with gray-green sagebrush and green-gray creosote. Occasionally, ten-foot-high Joshua trees rise out of the salt-encrusted earth, their trunks thick and scabrous and their arms twisted into comical shapes. On his first sight of these plants, the nineteenth century explorer John C. Fremont called them "the most repulsive tree in the vegetable kingdom." They are also among the oldest, and some of the big Joshua trees at Edwards may have been there when the Mimbrenos were still weaving floodgates out of yucca leaves and slapping mud onto the bottom of irrigation canals. Certainly these trees were quietly considering their cellular growth even as the Spanish conquered the land, the Mexicans wrested it from the Spanish, and the Americans took it from the Mexicans.

By the mid-twentieth century, the Joshua trees were in the middle of a new conquest and another frontier. In the Southwest, clean air, good weather, isolation, and large tracts of federal land promoted the growth of a high-tech industry that operated mainly in the sky. Of the many military bases in the desert, Edwards had an additional advantage; it possessed a unique runway—a dry lake bed with a surface naturally level and hard as rock. A fully loaded bomber might land there and depart, leaving only faint tire marks. Two or three times a year, rain filled the illusory lake with a foot of water which, with the ceaseless action of the winds, served only to resurface and reseal the ground.

As one might expect in the desert, life at Edwards could be intense. Simply changing one of the airplane's high pressure tires meant that a mechanic first rolled it into a steel cage which he hoped would protect him against any explosion. Checking the engine of the supersonic X-1 or X-2 was to risk another explosion or lethal spray of liquid nitrogen. Rather morbidly, the streets of the town, as well as the town itself, were named after pilots and crew members who had died. At the same time, in 1955 the maternity ward at the base produced six hundred babies—out of a population of fifteen hundred military wives.

By 1956, my father had spent over three thousand hours in the air and had flown all of the experimental, tricky Century Series jet fighters. In a profession that takes bravery for granted, he was known for being brave. As part of his job, he helped debug the F-100 by, as author Frank Harvey wrote, "inching steadily closer to the speed at which the plane went crazy." On another flight, he brought the multi-million-dollar F-105 back to base with a hazardous engine fire rather than abandon it. One test pilot put it in practical terms: "All the manufacturers used to ask for the guy with the bald head."

In the most dramatic story, my father pulled a fellow pilot out of a burning plane, despite the danger of the jet exploding. The pilot had landed and was trapped unconscious in the cockpit. "It was nothing but fire," Mel Apt would tell a reporter from *Life* magazine. "The only part I could see sticking out of the flames was the tip of the tail." On the dry lake bed that served as a runway, there were no stones or sticks with which to smash open the jammed Plexiglas canopy, and so my father beat on it first with his fists and then with a fifty-pound can of water. The canopy cracked and the pilot lived, although he lost both feet. My father received a medal. A few months later he was chosen to replace Pete Everest as one of the test pilots for the rocket-powered X-2. On his first flight in the X-2, the plane set a new speed record and went out of control. My father died in the crash.

I was two years old. In the same way that we know of the fluteplayer, I know of my father through artifacts that are sometimes ill-drawn and haphazardly preserved: parts of medals, letters, pictures, and sheets of clippings kept by my grandmother in leather-smelling scrapbooks. Here, in yellowed pages from *Reader's Digest* was an account of the pilot's rescue from the burning plane. This impressed me, for my grandparents had shelves of *Reader's Digest* and I knew the magazine to be an important adult icon. In other clippings, from the *Los Angeles Times,* the Tulsa *Daily World,* and the *Oregonian,* my father's life was couched in cliched and journalistic terms. He was "a member of an elite fraternity whose trademark is courage" and "whose job it is to roll back the frontiers of knowledge." He was a "cool head" and "an ace." He was also the "doomed pilot," "the fastest man in the world," "on his last ride."

As I read them at eight years of age, the words rang with complete authority. One account in the magazine *Cavalier* was particularly hardboiled. The author, who wrote that my father was a "quiet man, medium build, with very intense eyes," also explained the working conditions of a test pilot's job: "The deadly joker in supersonic flight is this: your X model starts out very well-behaved indeed. At a mere 760 miles an hour, the speed of sound, she is positively stable—a 'hands-off airplane.' So, you increase speed a little, and move up to 900 miles an hour. Now the airplane is neutrally stable. You have to fly her—and fly her carefully—every second. But you still are not satisfied, you hose more liquid oxygen out the tail pipe, and really start moving: 1,700 mph, say. Somewhere along the line, you have passed across the 'stability curve'—from safe neutral stability to deadly negative stability. There is now another guy riding in the jump seat: Death. Screw it up just a little and old buddy back there will grab the stick away from you and take over and he is a reckless sonofabitch. He doesn't give a damn for nothin'!"

If the legacy of magazines like *Cavalier* was tragic and singularly masculine, it was not the only legacy I had. Like the flute-player, the image of my father was a shifting one. My aunt remembered him as beloved younger brother full of funny tricks and mischief on the farm. My grandmother drew scenes of Depression-era Christmases in which the family was poor, virtuous, and content, stringing popcorn for the tree. (My grandmother promised each of her grandchildren a quilt if he or she didn't smoke cigarettes; in her innocence, she believed these patches of color could deter the pulse of adolescent rebellion. In the end, she made lots of quilts, even for those who did smoke.)

As a soldier in the Air Force, my father's nickname was Happy. As a husband, he helped my mother vacuum the house. In his off hours at the base—so went a piece in *Aviation Times*—he "paneled the den, put in a patio, and nursed along a striking flower garden."

In short, he was a nice man, a homebody, a man in touch with his feminine side. He was a man who came from the heartland, from Kansas and a childhood shot with gold. Kind as well as heroic, he was a man who played with his children, and in all the years of growing up without him, I never doubted that he would have loved me. More precisely, I never doubted that he did love me, and this love helped form the base on which I erected the structure of my life.

To complete the picture, my father—framed in his soldier's uniform in a photo set eternally on my mother's bureau—had one last and important virtue: he was touched by ordinariness. For publicity purposes, Bell Aircraft had a number of black and white glossies made of him throughout his career. Here he sits squeezed into the cockpit of the X-2, a scarf wrapped dashingly about his neck. Here he grins beside his plane and holds a space helmet with its dangling oxygen tube under one arm. In all of these photographs, my father looks distinctly un-Hollywood. He has my grandmother's round face. He is short. He is bald. He is an Everyman.

As I grew up, the sentimentalization of my father would have been complete were it not for rare sparks of reality thrown off by my mother. This might have happened more if my mother were the kind of woman who liked to talk about the past. She is, however, firmly rooted in present time and her silence concerning her only marriage, one that produced two children but lasted a short seven years, never seemed abnormal. Once, I remember her saying that my father loved to drink martinis. She may have noticed my surprised expression, for she went on to comment that my grandmother didn't know everything. Later I found a letter to my mother in which my father youthfully and crudely discussed sex. He also wrote about budgeting. And he assumed (cruelly, as I read it at the time) that the new baby, his second child, me, would be a boy.

Perhaps most revealing were the home movies he took, movies that my mother did not unearth until I was in college. In these, he panned quickly, perhaps selfishly, over friends and family to focus on what he loved best. Instead of shots of my mother as a young woman or of the two little girls who were my sister and I, we have a mini-documentary on what the sky looked like from an airplane window in 1955. (It looks much the same as today.) We can also watch clouds drift over the Grand Canyon and admire long desert vistas that cover many days of walking.

The central fact of my father's life remains that what he loved best killed him and that he chose, at some level, to die the way he did. Like other pilots, my father pleaded and worked for the chance to test the X-2, far and away the most difficult plane to fly at Edwards Air Force Base. Once hauled up by a Boeing B-50 and dropped like a bomb, the X-2 became the world's heaviest glider. When the rockets ignited and pushed it forward, the noise of the jet breaking the sound barrier could be heard for twenty miles. At that point the flight pattern was so complex it had to be worked out on a computer. If the plane climbed too steeply, the engines died. If it nosed down too sharply, it used too much of the ton of fuel it gulped per minute. In eight tries, pilot Pete Everest had only once come close to the planned pattern, when he set a speed record of 1,900 miles per hour. Once the plane was going this fast, there was always the chance of it somersaulting nose over tail in the high thin air that, without cabin pressurization, could boil a pilot's blood. In such high speed rolls, the plane had a number of aerodynamic quirks, such as control reversal. As the X-2 went faster, its instruments lagged behind its actual performance. And when its rockets finally stopped, they often did so with a semi-explosion or tail fire. At the end of the powered run, the plane glided again and had to be landed dead-stick on the packed desert sand.

Such a challenge was not assigned; it was coveted. "Here's to the lucky son of a gun who they let ride the X-2," went a party toast at one of the base's many parties. As that lucky man, Mel Apt was envied by his colleagues. On the very day of my father's first flight, the chase pilot Iven Kincheloe helped him into the skintight pressure suit and joked about locking him away so that he, Kincheloe, could fly the plane instead.

Although this was my father's first time in the X-2, he had flown "chase" behind it, ridden in the Boeing B-50 or mother plane, sat in the cockpit on the ground during engine warm-ups, studied movies of previous flights, talked with former test pilots, and operated a ground simulator with a stick and oscilloscope. This first trip was meant to be fairly routine, with vague orders to "stay within the envelope of knowledge." No speed limit was given, for the supervisors at Edwards felt my father would be better off not having to watch the machmeter (Mach I being the speed of sound). They also believed it was "a chance in a thousand" that a first-time pilot could fly the kind of pattern needed for high speeds.

In the cockpit of the X-2, in the belly of the B-50, my father and the crew ran through over seventy items on a check list: open line drain switch, retract air scoops, check pump number eleven, etc. This done, my father began the reverential countdown, "Five . . . four . . . three . . . two . . . one," and the captain of the B-50 pulled a handle beside his seat. On its thirteenth powered flight, the X-2 dropped into skies of deepest blue, skies that my father would not see since his concentration had to focus on the instruments before him.

Now everything seemed to go just right. The drop from the B-50 was perfect and Iven Kincheloe, following closely in the chase plane, yelled over the radio, "Suck your nose up now, Mel. That's a boy! Keep coming back!"

Next, with unusually good timing, my father fired off the two rockets. Flames trailed a hundred feet behind the X-2, and the plane flashed forward, leaving Kincheloe in his Sabrejet far behind. From the desert below, the plane's contrail of thick white moisture unfurled like a vaporish snake in the sky.

Then amazingly, as the X-2 zoomed upward, it stayed—for the first time ever—precisely on its planned flight pattern. Because my father had been told not to watch the machmeter, he may not have known how fast he was going. Still, at this point, a conservative pilot might have shut the rockets down, with the idea that the plane was close to exceeding its "envelope of knowledge." A conservative test pilot is an oxymoron, and my father rushed on to three times the speed of sound while the temperamental engines performed, again, exceptionally well—burning six seconds longer than ever before.

When the rockets died and the X-2 began to glide, it was farther away from the dry lake landing strip than on any previous run. As my father turned the plane, something went wrong. On the radio came the sound of a man slugged in the stomach. In the chase plane, Kincheloe was careening over the earth as he looked hard for the X-2. "Mel, Mel, do you read! Radar, do you have him?" he cried out. Confused, radar switched to Kincheloe's own plane and kept reporting his position. (Within a year, Iven Kincheloe would also die while testing a Lockheed Starfighter.) Meanwhile, the X-2 had fallen from 70,000 to 45,000 feet. Despite a tremendous buffeting, recorded by the cockpit's camera, my father was able to manually eject an escape capsule that blew him away from the main body of the plane. Partially based on this flight, later escape capsules would be fully automated. This one was not. Tumbling in the sky, moving in and out of consciousness, my father prepared to use the parachute.

Cavalier described the scene: "Here, then, is the terrible part. Apt was still conscious after his brutal supersonic tumble. He was putting up a frantic last-second fight for life. By examination of the wreckage, they established with certainty that Apt had been able to jettison his canopy, which gave him a free unhampered exit opening. He had also unfastened his seat belt. All he needed to do to complete the escape was stand up and pull the rip cord. Maybe five seconds would have made the difference. They were not given. The sand was coming up at him like a blazing yellow wall. Still in his seat, still conscious, fighting for his life to the very end, Captain Milburn Apt struck the desert."

I am now older than my father was when he crashed in the creosote and sage of the Mohave. As I age, he will stay thirty-two years old and become an increasingly complex figure. He will always remain the father to my child; when my sister and I refer to him in conversation, which is rarely, we use the word Daddy, for we are locked in that relationship. He is the man who once held me and who would have always loved me. He is the father a two-year-old would see, large and perfect and semi-divine. As I grew up and entered my twenties, he became something of a lover, and undoubtedly I chose my husband with my imaginary father in mind. Now in my thirties, I struggle a little to put aside these ideals and to see him as a peer—an imperfect parent like myself, a spouse who wrestled with sex and budgeting, a man who liked to drink but didn't tell his mother. As I grow even older, he will turn, I suppose, into the representation of youth. One day I will wake and find that he is my son.

Where he lives in my mind, of course, is in the desert. (I do not imagine him in rooms with furniture and TV sets.) He roams there, dressed as he was dressed for the photos in the newspaper clippings: a drab flight suit that resembles the overalls his own father used to wear, a scarf at the neck, a space helmet with its dangling oxygen tube. It is a vast land, this desert, and he can go anywhere. He has complete freedom. Perhaps that is why I love both him and the fluteplayer, for I know that they are exploring where I can not or would not. They wander an empty beautiful land full of surprises. They are merry, heroic, and human too. One is balding. One has a hump. One flies, on occasion, in a supersonic jet; now he can turn aside to look at the deep blue of the sky. One hunts mountain sheep with a bow and arrow. Although I know that there are other figures who live and connive within me, these are the two I know best, and I am grateful for their existence. They keep me company, and perhaps more than that, for their songs and ambitions are much wilder than my own. They know the power of myth. And as they walk through vistas of blazing sand, they search for forms of gold I have yet to imagine.

HOMEBIRTH

Her clinic is a tiny whitewashed adobe blazoned with turquoise paint on the door and window sills. Turquoise is a
popular color here in Silver City; in Mexican folklore, it has the
power to ward off witches. Outside, posted on the miniscule
lawn, a neat hand-lettered sign reads Licensed Midwife and then
again, underneath, *Partera Registrada*. Inside is a waiting room
with three chairs, a box of children's toys, and a decor that leans
toward primitive art. A large bulletin board shows a collage of
colorful snapshots: euphoric mothers holding newborn babies,
euphoric fathers holding newborn babies, babies themselves with
eyes squeezed shut and hands upraised in gestures of peace. In a
number of photos is the midwife herself, looking tired and
pleased.

I am here to pick up a friend, a fellow teacher, who is six
months pregnant. A former student of mine, Angelica Gutierrez,
waits on the chair beside me. I have been teaching writing skills
at the nearby university for nine years, and I see my former students everywhere: at the bank, at the grocery store, at the park
with our mutual children. I am not surprised now to see Angelica, and instead of flipping through the magazines provided, we
talk about her births.

In 1984 Angelica was sixteen when she had her first baby in the hospital. "Awful, awful, awful," she says of that. They didn't let her husband be with her during labor. They shaved her pubic hair. They took the baby away afterwards. When she was nineteen and pregnant again, Angelica couldn't afford to go to the hospital and so approached, with trepidation, a local midwife. Today Angelica is having her third child. Her husband's new insurance would cover a team of specialists. But Angelica is in love with the homebirth experience. Her friends think she is crazy. "Aren't you scared?" they ask. "No, I'm happy," she says. "Listen to me. This is wonderful."

Angelica's children are being born in the same house that their grandfather and great-uncles and great-aunts were born in. Up into the 1950s, most babies in Grant County were born at home, attended by a registered and licensed midwife. Thirty years later, homebirth accounts for only two percent of national births, a figure true for this area as well. In this clinic, the midwife averages two births a month, although she would like to do more. Her clients range from teenagers to thirty-five-year-old "teacher types." Forty percent are Hispanic, an ethnic group that makes up over 60 percent of the county's population. About half of her customers are on Medicaid. Of these, those who are having a homebirth only to save money almost always, the midwife says, find some last minute, last ditch way to the hospital.

In any discussion of homebirth, ideas of safety—"Aren't you afraid?"—usually come up. In New Mexico, the statistics of midwives and their homebirths are consistently better or similar to hospital births. Indeed, studies across the country and across the world confirm the reasonableness of having a baby at home; the World Health Organization has even urged the United States to support midwives as a way of reducing our high infant mortality rate. For people in the homebirth movement, this is all very old news. Safety is a priority. It is not, necessarily, the heart of the matter.

In 1984, the year Angelica went to the hospital for her first child, I was having my first child in an adobe house thirty miles from town. Like Angelica, I did not choose homebirth intuitively. In truth, I probably would not have had one if most of my friends had not. More bluntly, I did it because they did. Peer pressure may not seem a good reason for this or any decision of importance. In reality, it is exactly why we do so many important things, from getting married to wearing clothes on a hot summer's day. Normalcy is defined by what people are normally doing around you, and the majority of my friends—teacher types, ex-hippies, and one computer consultant—were birthing at home.

My acceptance of a homebirth was also influenced by my husband. Together, we had sweated and strained to build a single adobe room, fifteen-by-twenty feet large. We had made each brick, hammered in each nail, and rolled up the vigas onto the roof by the brute strength of our arms. Although the choice was mine to make, it was clear that a birth in this, our home, followed truly and cleanly from the vision that had brought us here.

A homebirth was another way of claiming this house and land as our own. It was a root sinking into the ground. It appealed to my husband's imagination, and in our constructed lives, imagination was a potent force.

Finally, not least, there was my midwife. As she had impressed Angelica on their first meeting, so she impressed me. She is a beautiful Anglo woman, with long golden hair and green eyes, who at the age of twenty-eight projected the authority of someone much older. Those who do not find beauty powerful are possibly around it too much or have never seen it at all. I don't know what this gift did to or for my midwife. I know only that she appeared tremendously competent, forthright, and self-assured. In her presence I felt it would be too gauche, too life-denying, to feel anything but trust in whatever she believed in. (I would realize, years later, that I had obscurely and pre-adolescently fallen in love with her.)

My midwife's assumption that I was also forthright, competent, and self-assured more or less corresponded with my own self-image. At the same time, I had doubts that I never revealed in our biweekly and then weekly sessions. There were moments in which I hoped for some physical problem that would rule out homebirth at the last minute. Under a licensed midwife, the list of these is long, for the integrity of homebirth lies in its restriction to a low-risk pregnancy. If, for example, my baby was too large, too small, too late, too early—then I would go to the hospital.

I had never stayed overnight in a hospital before. Now, suddenly, my picture of that experience grew increasingly benign. Hospital beds seemed so cool and inviting. Hospital white was such a clean color. I knew that such whiteness had its price. The most respected obstetrician in town had once smirked at me and let loose the Freudian slip, "I'd love to have your baby for you, Sharman." Still, secretly, I yearned to lay down the burden of having a child and to lay it precisely in the hands of someone who *was* paternal and overbearing. Let an obstetrician take the credit of birth, as long as he also took the blame. Let him lead me blindfolded through this valley of uncertainty. Let the drugs contract my uterus and the forceps extract the child. If the unspeakable happened, if horror struck and the baby died or was damaged, I believed—I rationalized—that I would be safer in the hospital. I did not mean physically. I meant emotionally. I would not have to feel as much there. A passive figure, wheeled on a metal table, strapped in, drugged, catheterized, fed through an IV, hooked to a machine: I would not be myself. I would not be responsible.

With inverse psychology, these feelings also led me home. The more I yearned for an outside authority, the more I guessed what was to be gained in not relinquishing my own. Something messy, bloody, and intensely personal lay ahead. It must be important if I was afraid of it. It must be, I reasoned, too important to give away.

Desired and even orchestrated, my first pregnancy had its share of inauspicious omens. As I drove home with the good news, a truck turning left accordioned my fender into the passenger's seat. Three days later, a doctor gave me Progesterone to "prevent

miscarriage." In my vulnerable state, I still roused myself to protest. "Don't take it," the man said classically, "if you don't care
about your baby." Soon after I learned that Progesterone was a
known cause of birth defects. When I rushed to confirm this with
another doctor, he spoke of "heart holes" and "limb reductions"
and noted, in a kindly way, that his office did abortions. My third
appointment was with a specialist who dismissed the whole affair.
In his opinion, if my husband and I were not willing to risk this
pregnancy, we were not willing to risk pregnancy at all.

At this point, four weeks after conception, I settled into being
an expectant mother. My initiation was fairly typical. Most pregnant women I know have either had a true scare or have concocted
one. Growing a baby is the most exotic of lands, bordered by joy,
fraught with a sense of danger, and beset by internal politics.
Nine months is barely enough time for us to drain these emotions
to their last bittersweet dregs. By the end, discomfort compels
us. Like adventurers cast on some Pacific isle, we are ready to sail
back to civilization.

Thirty-year-old women often have a long first labor, and I was
no exception. The amniotic sac ruptured at four o'clock Tuesday
morning and as I jumped from the bed to let the water gush from
my body, I felt very young, like a child who had gotten up too
early on Christmas. For two weeks, I had kept prepared the bag
of things my midwife required of me. These included disposable
surgical gloves, a bottle of Betadine, a suction for the baby's nose,
a thermometer, a large pan, sanitary napkins, three towels, three
sheets, and a dozen clean rags. The last three items had to be
sterilized, a feat accomplished by placing them in a brown paper

bag in a hot oven for two hours. The "sterilization" lasted two weeks, and I had re-sterilized everything a few days ago. Smugly, a good girl, I returned to bed and a fitful sleep.

In the morning, I called my midwife. By late afternoon she had arrived with her assistant, also a licensed midwife, in a big red van. As the summer evening darkened our south-facing wall of windows, my contractions began seriously. By nine o'clock, they lasted a minute and were two to three minutes apart. My husband set out dinner, a friend came over to help, music was played, and happy talk eddied about the room. I began to pace up and down from the bed to the table to the rocking chair that symbolized our future. My route followed no particular pattern but traced the cement grouting of a floor covered with yellow and orange Mexican tile. As each contraction heightened, my steps slowed, and I counted the tiles, and counted my steps.

By midnight, people were taking shifts. My midwife was herself seven months pregnant and had fallen asleep in the big red van. Her assistant lay on a cot outside, under the dramatic sweep of the Milky Way. Earlier she had impressed us by picking out constellations like Perseus and Lacerta. For three hours, my friend stayed with me and then woke my husband who, for the rest of the night, read aloud *The Yearling* by Marjorie Kinnan Rawlings. I listened to his voice, not the words, and continued to pace the floor, slowly, slavishly, like some ancient Chinese woman with bound feet.

Tedium is a word to describe that labor. The contractions went on, and on, a kneading and cramping meant to stretch and pull open the circular muscles around the cervix. This dilation, measured in centimeters, is complete at the magical number of ten: at that point, the baby is ready to be pushed down the birth canal. Periodically through the night, the midwife or her assistant would check the baby's heartbeat with a stethoscope on my belly. They also checked inside me for an update on the cervix, and for most of that interminable Wednesday, the update was disappointing. At 1:00 A.M., I was three centimeters. At 7:00 A.M., I was four.

At that time, our little adobe had no hot water, and as a way of "making it happen" we all trooped over to a neighbor's house so that I could take a shower and enema. Now, in the few minutes between contractions, I dozed in the hallucinatory way that causes the head to snap upright just as the soul touches the coastline of sleep. There in the shower I saw the pink porcelain tile come alarmingly close. I snapped awake and did not fall. A few hours later, back home again, I had dilated to five.

It was a bold bright afternoon and the southern glass wall of which we were so proud framed the lengthening shadows of yuccas on grama grass. My water had broken a day and a half before, and I had been in moderate to hard labor for fifteen hours. I asked my midwife why it was taking so long. She may have replied that a mother can lengthen labor out of fear or rejection of the child. More probably, she did not say this at all. More probably, it was only an idea rattling about in my head, and I suspected, in the heads of those around me. It was an idea that made me angry. I wasn't afraid! I wanted the baby! I asked my midwife if there was something I could do.

"Get mad," she suggested. "Tell your body you're ready."

That fit my mood well and so I began to mutter, "I'm mad! I'm ready!" as I wandered in my slow and crazy way about the room.

Next I asked the midwife if crying ever helped.

"Oh yes," she assured me, brightening a little. We were both lovers of strategy—of scientific reasoning, technique, and causation. Who knew what chemicals a good cry might stimulate?

Strategically then, my husband and I went off for a car ride on the bumpy road that leads from our house to the black-topped highway. When we reached its flat expanse, we went on driving and in the car, between contractions, as the scenery unrolled, I cried.

In hindsight, the comic moment occurred when we stopped at a trailhead into the Gila National Forest and Gila Wilderness Area. The path follows the sparkling Sapillo Creek, and my husband thought that a short hike along this creek, in the beauty of the woods, would be a good idea. Protesting, I stumbled from the car and leaned heavily on his arm. As we hobbled a few steps down the path, a backpacker emerged from what must have been a first trip or a long one. Spying us, he broke into a grin. We were the first human beings he had seen for days, and eagerly he began the hail-well-met exchange that hikers luxuriate in. He did not get the expected reply. Instead, a huge woman moaned in his face, turned her husband around, and labored back to the car before ever reaching the scenic Sapillo. The backpacker's face remains with me today: young, acne marked, shocked at my inappropriateness.

An hour later, at the house, the midwife's assistant lay tanning on her cot and flipping the last pages of a murder mystery. The midwife sat inside, doing nothing, in a straight-backed chair. She had circles under her eyes, and her own pregnant stomach bloomed uncomfortably beneath her folded hands. "You know," she said, as I began once more to whine and pace the floor. "The pains are only going to get worse."

I stared at her, devastated. They were? At that moment they felt pretty bad. Was this a hint? A move to the hospital? The latter had not occurred to me, for my doubts about homebirth had vanished at the onset of a labor that was long and tedious but never fearful. Now I felt admonished and betrayed. "I'm really mad now," I muttered to my body, to my uterus, to the baby itself. "I'm really ready!"

Later still, we checked my dilation. By this time, I think, I was too tired to feel hopeful. "Oh, you're going to love this," the midwife said. The room's ceiling of pine vigas glowed with the golden light of freshly cut wood. In fact, the ceiling always glowed like this but I rarely noticed it. "You're at nine centimeters. You're almost there!" She laughed, I laughed, and suddenly everyone but me began to move with a bustle and wonderful sense of purpose. Water started boiling. I heard the joyful clink of instruments. I got up from the bed, but no. For the first time, after twenty hours of walking, I wanted only to lie down. From the windows I could see the tip of Cooke's Peak turning to lavender. The hills below were silhouetted against a royal blue in which a single planet shone. Another evening, another night, was at hand.

It took an hour more of waiting and three of pushing before anyone was born. In that time, I learned a lot. As a child, I had never been an athlete in competitive sports, had never understood about concentration or team effort. Once in the sixth grade I did make the "B" team, where my idea of playing baseball was to daydream in the outfield until the ball came to me, by which time it was almost always too late to catch it. In my twenties, for exercise, I became a runner and let my mind and body go their separate ways. Now, here, lying naked in a quilted bed, was what I imagined the best kind of athleticism to be about—about pushing yourself to the limit, about believing in yourself, trying again, moving through the pain, listening to your coach, and trying again.

You can do it! The baby was posterior, lying against my back, and that made it harder. You can do it! I had no urge to push, I didn't know how, and that made it harder. You can do it! My squad of cheerleaders—midwife, assistant, husband, friend—rallied me again and again with that cry. You can do it, they said, and when they forgot to cheer me on, I reminded them to, for I depended on their enthusiasm. I followed their instructions. I used their energy. This was a group effort and, for the first time in my life, I was at the center of it. I was the focal point, concentrating, intent, working, only sometimes scared. Can I do it? I asked them. You can, they said. And I did. It felt great. (My husband has his own story to tell. The pine vigas glowed. Darkness lapped at the window. He had never felt so connected to his life.)

As seven pounds of newborn spilled into the world, I heard the assistant say "It's a blondie!" and then, in a moment, "Oh, what a temper." Gently, they put the amazingly solid baby on my stomach. My husband and I drew close together and stared: our daughter looked floppy, distracted, radiantly pink. It was one minute past midnight, slightly chilly, and someone bundled her into a blanket. My husband cut the cord and we squabbled briefly over who would hold her first. "Maria!" I breathed into her tiny ear. She turned to me, dazed and uncomprehending. Then she held still and took my breast.

As the placenta slithered out, the midwife kneaded my stomach. When I continued to bleed, she gave me a shot of Pitocin to control hemorrhage. By then, the baby had already been given its one and five minute rating on the Apgar scale, where she scored high. As in a hospital, silver nitrate would be applied to her eyes to prevent infection and she would be given a dose of Vitamin K. Because I am RH negative, a sample of the cord blood would be sent to the hospital. Meanwhile the midwife was sewing up a small tear in my perineum, and my friend, as she is wont to do, went quietly about the business of washing dishes and cleaning house. My husband sat and rocked his child. Outside, the darkness had the eerie expectant sheen of early morning. The birds were still asleep. The birth was over. I felt tremendously energized.

The word *midwife* literally means "with woman" and this quality of withness is perhaps the midwife's greatest virtue. Withness implies empathy, equality, and, in practical terms, a willingness to stay with a laboring mother for as long as it takes. During Hippocrates' time, in Western society, midwives were an honored class. But in the Dark Ages, this feminine profession became increasingly devalued. The idea that witches, acting as midwives, killed unbaptized babies and used them in Satanic rites seemed logical to the Church. As potential sources of birth control and abortion techniques, midwives were doubly damned—and occasionally burned.

By the sixteenth century, tradesmen called barber-surgeons were being brought in for cases of obstructed childbirth. These men brought a bag of perforators and metal hooks used to drag a child from the womb whole or piecemeal. The later refinement of forceps was a major breakthrough in obstetrics. But like other tools of science they were seen as distinctly masculine. At this point, the use of instruments in delivery can be seen as a rough dividing line, with women on one side and men on the other.

The rest of Western midwifery is marked by a struggle between the sexes to gain control of the birth process. By 1850, a part of life historically dominated by women was being successfully usurped. At first, midwives fought back, accusing doctors even then of using instruments unnecessarily to avoid "the onerous chore of staying up throughout the night." Playing hardball, they also brought in the specter of lust: what other motive could explain such "frequent examinations with the finger and the hand?" In response, physicians encouraged the idea that even a normal delivery was so dangerous as to override any embarrassment, suspicion, or pain on the part of the patient. By the twentieth century, pregnancy had evolved, philosophically, into a life-threatening disease.

Starting in the 1920s with the beatific-sounding Twilight Sleep—morphine followed by a hallucinogen coupled with ether or chloroform—mothers could be completely removed from the birth of their children. In 1950, my mother fondly remembers being given a shot, blankness, and then waiting in bed while the nurses took care of my sister. For other women, the hospital experience was anything but beatific, and the horror stories of these years are well known: the isolation of labor, the leather straps, the high metal stirrups. In this setting, the woman was seen, from a technician's point of view, as a birthing machine that required service. Usually the machine also required tinkering. Oxytocyn to start up a "slow" uterus, pain relievers to ease the artificial and unnaturally strong contractions, synthetic hormones again as the drugs impaired the mother's ability to push. Babies were born "blue" from a drug-induced lack of oxygen. The Cesarean rate skyrocketed. And in 1980, American hospitals had more infant deaths due to birth injuries and respiratory diseases than almost any other industrialized nation.

There was opposition. As we learned about the dangers of drugs, both mothers and doctors came to see them as less desirable. Husbands and family members were allowed in the delivery room. Certain medical routines—induced labor, intravenous feeding, and the episiotomy—became less routine. In remote areas, progress, as usual, moved in fits and starts. Still, in 1987 when I was pregnant with my second child, a progressive family-care doctor had just opened her office, nurse-midwives worked at the hospital, and the hospital itself touted a "birthing room" with homey atmosphere and wooden cradle for the baby. Even the most respected obstetrician in town had adopted a different, if still paternal, stance. One friend reported with dismay that he would not let her have the painkiller she requested. "Wait it out," he cajoled her cheerfully. "Just a few more minutes. You can do it."

In part because my options were greater, my decision to have a second homebirth was not automatic. In some ways I felt more conservative than before and, to my surprise, so did my midwife. After three more years of catching babies, she had a greater respect for her relationship to statistics. If only 1 percent of mothers hemorrhage dangerously after labor, the midwife who sees a hundred mothers will see the one who does. If only a fraction of cords are looped too tightly about the baby's neck, it's still a significant number; in one year my midwife had three such babies. That she could handle these emergencies was not in question. But her natural optimism had tempered, and she no longer did births more than twenty minutes from the hospital. For my husband and me, she would make an exception. But she also suggested we have the birth in town, at a friend's house, say, or—as one couple did—at a nearby hotel.

This time, my husband and I even visited the hospital's new birthing room. There was nothing wrong with it, exactly. The pink pillows matched the pink coverlet, the baby's cradle had been varnished to a shine, and a poster of trees covered one entire wall. Best of all, as the nurse showed us, was the mechanical bed that rose up and down and let the woman actually sit up during delivery. In the tour, we went on to examine the traditional labor room next door. Here was the flat white table with its heavy stirrups, surrounded by the decor of machinery and plastic. Of course, our guide said, there was no guarantee I would get the birthing room. I would get on a list, and it was first-come, first-served. There was no guarantee I would not wind up flat on my back on the white table, a position which, short of being hanged upside down, is perhaps the worst one for delivery. There was no guarantee I would get the pink coverlet.

In the end, as I went home and thought about it, the pink coverlet didn't even look that good. Naturally I would come to the hospital if I needed to. I would even have the birth in town so as to be closer to its services. But as for the bed that rose up and down—as though I couldn't rise up and down by myself! as though the privilege of being able to sit up was the best I could hope for, a privilege granted by the pulleys of a mechanical bed— as for first-come, first-served and stirrups to place my feet, no, I thought, not for me. I was grateful for the hospital. It was an important aid to birth. But it was not a replacement.

My intuition, at long last, had started to kick in.

In retrospect, it seems my ambiguity concerning homebirth vanished for the rest of that pregnancy. In truth, I don't think it did until the beginning of labor. Then, as before, all my doubts disappeared and I was where I needed to be, focusing on the task at hand.

In this birth, events moved so rapidly that my focus blurred a little. Labor started with strong contractions at 12:30 A.M. and ended with a ten-pound baby boy six hours later. In this birth, I didn't try to be stoic. This one hurt more. This time, too, my husband's and midwife's reassurances rang a bit perfunctory. We were all surprised at the speed of dilation. We were all a bit more businesslike and a bit less magical. No golden *vigas* glowed over our heads, for we were at a friend's house, in a modern room with walls made of sheetrock. This time, when the baby's large head began to crown, I screamed in outrage. I hollered out my midwife's name, not caring who heard me or what they might think. My friend, her husband, their two young sons, and my three-year-old daughter were sitting in the middle of the room, watching me with considerable interest. Something in their position, crosslegged on the floor, made me feel like a television set. In a small but well-lit clearing of my mind, I realized that I had a choice. I could grit my teeth or scream unbecomingly. What does it matter? I remember thinking. Perhaps in this instance, screaming was the better strategy.

After all the fuss, our son emerged with a headful of brown hair and a mouth screwed only slightly in irritation. His Apgar scores were nearly perfect, his wrists and ankles rolled with fat. Flopped on my stomach, he stared up at me peacefully in the morning light. For a few minutes, the assistant took the baby and busied herself verifying his patently healthy condition.

Peacefully I delivered the placenta and continued to bleed. My midwife gave me a dose of Pitocin and then another. Because large babies are associated with diabetes, she also telephoned our pediatrician. Outside the window, the sky trailed banners of celebratory pink. Relieved and euphoric, I submitted to the medical procedures: my blood pressure taken, some slight stitching up. Because I had hemorrhaged, the midwife measured the iron in my blood with a small hand-held device, and my husband was impressed with this bit of gadgetry. Within an hour, a friend came by and took pictures. In all of these, my daughter holds her new brother. While the rest of us look obediently at the camera, she and he gaze with complete concentration into each other's eyes.

My daughter is nearly five now. Recently, in a seminar at work, I was asked to remember a time when I had felt powerful. Instantly I saw Maria's birth. I did not, of course, see a baby's head crowning. Instead I saw my own naked thighs and knees spread unnaturally apart. I saw, at the periphery of vision, the blurred hands and faces of my husband and friends. I saw the colors of my grandmother's quilt glowing intensely. It seemed that one of my legs was streaked with blood. It would seem that I had never been so vulnerable, so dependent in all my life. Yet I remember this, a physical memory, lodged deep in the body, as a moment of power. In my second homebirth, I remember as well the unabashed decision to shriek. I remember, still, feeling at the center.

As my friend emerges from her appointment with the midwife, I say goodbye to Angelica Gutierrez. I also say hello to the midwife, who stops to tell me about a homebirth-related case headed for the Supreme Court. This class action suit will determine if women have a constitutional right to choose their place of giving birth and if midwives have a constitutional right to practice their profession. My midwife is passionate about the subject. So am I. It appalls me that homebirth is illegal in some states. I am aghast that Arizona midwives can not carry Pitocin. All of us, all the women in this room, feel the flare of anger. It dies quickly and, eager to start their private communion, the midwife and Angelica disappear into the office.

On my way out, I touch the door and tell my friend that turquoise is the color to ward off witches. "Oh," she says, lulled and euphoric by her visit to the midwife, "it's my favorite color too."

Her big belly, taut and firm, pushes out into the late afternoon air. Life is swimming inside her. A child dreams beneath the skin. Briefly she rests a hand on the highest point of her curved stomach, where I would like, very much, to put my hand as well.

TRADING POSTS

T he Indian trader at Two Grey Hills seems morose. His Navajo wife left two years ago, and the new Thriftway store on Highway 666 is cutting into his business. Six miles west of that highway, on a rutted dirt road, the Two Grey Hills Trading Post overlooks a deep wash that irregularly rages with water. It is dry now. As if to make up for this lack, the landscape flows out like an ocean or immense lake, 360 degrees of chalky brown and white desert, with a few sculpted hills and a scattering of vegetation. To the west, the Chuska Mountains with their folds of blue spruce and fantastically eroded sandstone rise with distant authority. Gallup, New Mexico is an hour's drive south and Shiprock a half hour north. For the last sixteen years, the trader has lived in such remote parts of the Navajo reservation: first Shonto, then Pinon, and now Two Grey Hills.

His face lightens as he introduces his sons, good-sized friendly boys who are probably about twelve and fourteen. We pass through the store with its shelves of groceries, tools, mops, and hanging ropes of wool. In the back, behind a locked door, is the small rug room. The trader relaxes and even smiles as he picks up a rug, made by weaver Ramona Curley.

Historically, the Navajos here have always disliked dyes and colored cloth. Early traders couldn't even sell their red calico. Gradually, the use of all natural wool—white, grey, tan, and brown—woven with an outside black border and geometric interior became the Two Grey Hills trademark. Chinle, Crystal, Ganado, Two Grey Hills: Navajo weaving styles are really a listing of trading posts where ambitious traders worked to influence design and color. In the 1910s, the Two Grey Hills trader would spend hours with a weaver, pointing out defects or praising a certain line. An attention to the quality of weaving emerged, and today a Two Grey Hills work is considered the "Cadillac" of Navajo rugs.

Ramona Curley has been weaving since she was a girl, seventy years ago. While many Navajo rugs are now made of commercially dyed and machine spun yarn, Ramona still uses the wool from her family sheep. After the spring shearing, the heavy animal hair must be washed clean again and again, carded, and handspun. For a tighter yarn and weave, the wool is spun twice or even three times. It will take at least six months before a rug like the one I am looking at is ready. Ramona likes the Two Grey Hills trader, and he likes her, and she brings her weavings here out of loyalty and friendship. He gives her a good price and pays her immediately— the Navajos, he says, do not work on commission. In return, she buys her groceries at the post: some Bluebird flour, canned goods, and coffee.

Perhaps another year will pass before the right, well-off, adventuresome tourist will travel six miles of dirt road to the trading post. Ushered into the rug room, the tourist will fall in love with the classic Two Grey Hills pattern. Again, the trader gives a good price—$3,500 for a weaving 42 by 63 inches. The same weaving, the trader says, would cost five or six thousand in a Scottsdale shop. The tourist is happy and not only with the sales tag. He knows that the rug is genuine, locally made. He also knows something of what that means. He remembers passing sheep with their horns painted red (he never learned why); he remembers the trader's voice as they stood together on the weatherbeaten porch—"God, it's been dry. The wash hasn't even run. Is it bad where you are?" As the tourist leaves the post, the colors of the land are the colors of his new rug, and later he will see and remember Shiprock, the great volcanic prow rising out of the earth, landlocked, impossible.

The trader goes on to tell me that one woman "from Maine or maybe New Hampshire" has come to Two Grey Hills to buy rugs from three generations of Curley weavers: Ramona, her daughter, and her granddaughter. "That's special, isn't it?" the trader asks rhetorically. I have to step back to look up at him, for the trader is tall. I am beginning to see that behind his lugubrious mask is a wealth of pride.

Not all the rugs in this room fetch $3,500. Not all are traditional or as good as Ramona's. The trader shows me a smaller weaving for a few hundred dollars. It, too, uses the handspun wool, but the texture is rough and the design less appealing. "This lady here has been weaving a long time," the trader notes. "But she never got any better. And she never will. Still, she needs encouragement because she's using the old ways. Her work is handspun."

Encouragement has always been a part of the trader's stock. It sounds paternalistic. Certainly it veered into bullying, at least as much bullying as the Navajos would allow, which was probably not much. Even some of the early weavers could never be "encouraged" to repeat a design in a rug, no matter how lucrative such mass marketing might be. To these artists, the weaving was like a painting, a one-shot love affair. For other Navajos, the making of rugs, baskets, or jewelry was tied more practically to livelihood. The trader's encouragement, in terms of the quality of wool or which design and color to use, was based on his commercial interests—on selling the product to the Anglo world. That was the Navajo's interest as well, and out of this came a home business that allowed a rural people to stay in their hogans and canyons and still make money.

"There wouldn't be weaving now," the trader at Two Grey Hills declares, "if there hadn't been trading posts and traders. They kept it alive in the twenties and thirties and forties when no one else cared, when it was just an Indian blanket bought by the pound."

From another viewpoint, traders were forced to accept their weavers' rugs so as to keep trade flowing. They weren't always happy about it. Writing about her life in the 1920s, Shonto trader Elizabeth Hegemann complained about the "thousands of pounds of rugs which we had to buy even though we had no retail outlet." Like other traders, she flinched when certain unskilled weavers brought rugs into her post.

Today, Navajo crafts may be the largest cottage industry in the United States. In the 25,000-square-mile reservation, an estimated 12,000 women and 25 men weave commercially. About 7 percent of these are more artist than artisan, adding to the traditions even as they master them. At the lower end of the scale, prices remain affordable. At the top of the line, rugs sell for over $50,000.

Such rugs and prices are fabulous concoctions of the desert. They are not really what interest me about trading posts. What interests me is what the women say, women like Mary Jeanette Kennedy who traded for thirty years at Salina Springs, Chinle, and Rock Springs.

"Every day seemed to be an adventure in itself," jubilated this city girl from the South. On her first journey to the Navajo reservation in 1913, she found the weird erosions and scalloped bluffs of Salina Springs to be inexpressively beautiful. Her memories of her life there are concrete and sensual: "I was alone and bathing the baby in a small tub near the kitchen fire" or "Never have peaches tasted any better to us than the ones from Canyon de Chelly."

At the Shonto Trading Post, Elizabeth Hegemann, too, found herself extraordinarily content, sheltered in a tree-lined canyon below pink mesas and a vista that could make your chest feel hollow, your bones lighten. Both these women worked hard: shifting cases of canned goods, hoisting bags of pinon nuts, manhandling broken trucks, haggling over pawn tickets, exchanging flour for wool. Their living quarters were primitive, their husbands often tactiturn. Yet they perceived their lives as special. They relished the beauty of Hopi Snake dances and "the sound of the Evening Song rising skyward." In some ways they had the best of two worlds. Their days, as Elizabeth Hegemann wrote, were work filled and sun drenched, "a part of the Navajo land with its absorbing daily routine." Their nights were often gay with the talk of cultured visitors: a parade of movie stars, artists, and academics vying to participate in an exotica so close to home.

As I read the memoirs left by these women, I feel envious and then suspicious. Where are the lice? The drunks? The racism? The long marital quarrels in a long winter?

I am perversely glad to find some of these things in the letters of Hilda Faunce, written in 1914. "The barrenness, the vastness threatened me," she confessed to her sister as her husband coaxed their horse drawn wagon across northern Arizona. Her honesty is revealed in the verb, and her years at the Covered Waters trading post are checkered with a sense of poverty and hardship. A cyclone gruesomely kills two young boys herding sheep. Entire families die from influenza. The Navajos rise in mutiny at the draft of World War I. Faunce herself acclimatizes slowly. With unconscious prejudice, she titles a later book chapter "Indian Ways and Wiles." Humor is her saving grace. On one weary trip to get a supply of small pox vaccine, the Navajo driver is forced to bear down hard on the recalcitrant horses. "For awhile I was fairly sick with the whipping," Hilda begins softly. "Then I regretted I hadn't brought a pitchfork."

All that was nearly a hundred years ago. As my husband and I drive through the Navajo reservation—our small children in the backseat amid a litter of food, drink, and toys—I can see the obvious ways in which trading posts have changed. Barter is no longer allowed. Cash (and the odd Master Charge) is the rule. Mobility has freed the Navajo to seek the best market; if a weaver does not like the prices at Two Grey Hills, she'll hop in her pickup truck and drive on to Gallup. If she is one of the best, she'll send her rugs directly to galleries or her own agent. The custom of pawning jewelry is now discouraged by reservation laws. And since small posts near towns can not compete with supermarkets, many have closed or become convenience stores, a place to pick up a video or soda.

Still, a trader like the one at Two Grey Hills thinks of himself as traditional, in service as well as trading. Unlike a convenience store, he extends credit, a lot of credit, to his customers. He also acts as a banker. "Around the first of the month, when the Social Security and SSI checks come in, we cash them in quantities outside business people wouldn't believe," he says emphatically. His pride shows strongly here, for in other ways the trader knows that most business people would not consider him much of a businessman. He is, perhaps, too free with his time and his services. He is too much a part of a community that is too poor. "Selling rugs is a sideline," he tells me, "but from October to March, I don't see white people. The bulk of what I do is everyday trade."

We come out of the rug room to rejoin my husband, son, and daughter on the porch. I sense that my husband is eager to leave. This is our first family trip, and driving from trading post to trading post, from candy bar rack to candy bar rack, is not the best trip to take preschool children on. My son begins to shriek at his sister for touching his hair.

Meanwhile, the trader says he'd like to promote his store a little more. He'd like to see more tourists come down that dirt road. He also warns that "Navajos don't like loudmouths. They don't like loud voices. They think that's very rude. If you act dignified and quiet, you'll get more respect than the people who come in with their cameras and shorts, making a lot of noise."

The noise of my children seems to intensify. Somewhat abashed, I do not look down at the shorts I am wearing. It is the middle of summer, and our car is not air conditioned. I have traveled a fair amount in foreign countries, covering my legs and arms and head whenever it seemed necessary. But it had not occured to me to think like that, like a foreigner, in a seven hour drive from my home in southwestern New Mexico. It had not occured to me that on Highway 666, from Gallup to Shiprock, I was, in effect, entering another country.

From Two Grey Hills, we drive another five miles to the relative lushness of Toadlena. There the windows of the trading post, a massive stone building, are covered with plywood and obviously the place is closed. (We learn later that it is not.) Nearby, a small adobe village has sprung up around a spring and the Toadlena Boarding School, with its more modern, cheap-looking construction. On the road, we see a sign pointing to a fish hatchery.

Behind us, the mountains are a comforting brown wall, while the vista east is long, spacious, and delicately colored. The trees and gardens that accompany human life look seductively green. The air smells good. Perhaps it is the smell of wild honey locust. Perhaps it is the smell of sage. Whatever it is, there is a sweetness to this village and to this view, and my husband and I begin a conversation we have had many times.

"Could you live here?" he asks. "Could you live here?"

I consider it. We are both drawn to places that balance beauty and remoteness. Like traders, we are drawn to the lonely introspection of living in countries different from our own. Like everyone, we are looking for a way to make our lives special.

"Yes," I say and mean it. I imagine my soul would swell with the emptiness that surrounds Toadlena. I imagine I would grow more full. I would see more clearly what I am in the contrast of what I am not.

Then, as usual, I amend what I have said.

"For a few years."

Sanostee is our next stop, and I would not have thought from its rustic wood corrals and peeling storefront that, like thirty other reservation posts, it is now owned by Thriftway. A sign on the store window, "No Loitering," does give me pause. Loitering was an art and a right in the historic trading posts and seemed to fit the ambiance of Two Grey Hills as well. I find the manager, an older Anglo man with a pleasant face and pencil thin moustache, and tell him I am writing about modern day trading posts. He smiles a little wildly. He informs me that the store now offers more to Navajos than ever before; its hours have been extended to Sunday and to nine every night. I can see, too, that with Thriftway's backing, the post is well-capitalized and fully stocked. The shelves fairly bulge and the products leap out at the consumer just as they are supposed to. The manager also tells me that he gives credit to customers. Later, however, he indicates that Thriftway's goal is to "purge" the current credit list to something more businesslike. "Well, of course," he looks away, "the old trader who lived here, he knew everyone. He had been here for years and years and years."

When the manager's wife arrives, the manager bolts like a housecat waiting for an open door. The wife, on the other hand, is eager to chat. She says that the story of her life would be a blockbuster, and she gives me a few examples. She says that she also writes and plans to give the local Indians, whom she describes as "destitute," the proceeds of her first published book. She explains that she and her husband have been here a year and are about to be transferred to a bigger, better Thriftway store.

In the bathroom, another sign reads, rudely to my eye, "Clerks who have been cashing checks have been cashing them WRONG." The sign goes on to enumerate, at length, what kind of checks the clerks may not cash. I am beginning to dislike Sanostee. After buying a lunch of microwaved burritos and Kraft cheese, of fruit juice for the kids and coffee for me, we drive up to the mesa that looks down over the trading post and its oasis of cottonwoods.

The sun is hot enough to add to my crankiness. The children are asleep, and this does not fit with my plan to have them sleep later and more conveniently. My husband walks beside the car, up and down, waving his arms with all the greed of our daughter on an Easter egg hunt. Fossils cover the ground. Everywhere, in slabs of limestone, swirl the stony remains of ancient oysters and sinuous shipworms. Some hundred million years ago, this mesa was part of a shallow sea that stretched from the Gulf of Mexico to Canada, soaking up heat and distributing it so that magnolia trees could grow in Greenland and dinosaurs live north of the Arctic Circle. Right here, where my husband walks, sharks swam and snapped at the stray turtle, crocodilian, or scaly garfish. Right here, plesiosaurs and mosasaurs paddled in the warm water. At the close of the Cretaceous Period, sixty-five million years ago, the retreat of this great sea, with the resulting changes in climate and environment, helped bring about the death of these big reptiles. My husband calls out his excitement to me. Time. Timelessness. Extinction. The constant metamorphosis: seas to mesas, animals to stone.

On Highway 666 again, we cruise up to the reservation town of Shiprock and the big mercantile trading posts there. The Shiprock Trading Post is a bustling well-lit place, half supermarket, half department store, full of Navajo customers. There is a special this week on disposable diapers and two kinds of yogurt competitively priced. There is also a display that sells yarn for weavers and tools for silversmiths. Presumably, the people who buy these things also return with their own work, for crafts are still a big part of this store. The jewelry cases shine with polishing. The rug room is huge and dramatically lit, with a high ceiling and solid pine *vigas*. Although the post sells mainly to wholesalers, the Navajo clerk who takes me around is solicitous and clearly willing to make a deal. Behind the store, I can see barns full of hay and sturdy corrals where bawling sheep are brought each spring to be trucked to market.

The Shiprock Trading Post is a healthy evolution of the old-time store. In their own way, so are the big lodges like Gouldings at the border of Utah and Thunderbird in the mouth of Canyon de Chelly. Both these resort hotels began as isolated trading posts. Now, they trade in tourists, and you are as likely to hear German as Navajo. Because these resorts have the money for historic renovation, they can be impressive. At Cameron, the grand-nephew of the original owner has spent over a million dollars restoring the 45-room motel and restaurant. He is also bringing to life the famous terraced gardens, whose alien green symmetry must be nurtured carefully in the dead heat of the Painted Desert.

Other posts retain a dilapidation that seems equally nurtured—and as historic. The corrals at Salina Springs stand knock-kneed with the force of the sly, artistic wind. Near Little Black Spot Mountain, Pinon Post is a faded store that trades, nonetheless, with more than 150 weavers who bring in rugs for the wholesalers who come through. In Utah, the Oljeto Trading Post is a slow-motion collapse of mud and wood. Inside, the post assumes credibility with the now rare bullpen where customers stand in front of high counters and point to goods stacked precariously to the ceiling: canned food, medicine, a sewing machine, fan belts, bolts of cloth, videos, and tires. Another original bullpen is at the Hubbells Trading Post, a National Historic Site cleverly leased by the Park Service to an experienced trader.

There are those who think that isolated and working posts like Pinon, Shonto, Oljeto, and Two Grey Hills will eventually disappear. Only Hubbells will remain, a showcase to tradition. The trader at Two Grey Hills disagrees.

"The ones that are already closed, and that's maybe half or more of the ones that ever were, they're gone and gone for good," he says. "But the ones that are left serve a need other kinds of stores just don't. They're still kicking. They always will be."

After Shiprock, my husband and I are ready to go home. Still, as we hurry down State Highway 44, we take the last, mandatory, serendipitous turn. We slow for another dirt road and a sign that announces the Carson Trading Post. Stokes Carson started this off-the-reservation post in 1918 and lived here with his wife and four daughters for most of his life. Like other traders, he worked a lot with sheep—buying, selling, cross-breeding, shearing, dipping whole herds in vats of calcium sulfide to kill mites, ticks, and the parasite that causes scabies. The land around the Carson Trading Post is flat and white, with afternoon haze hiding the mountains I know must be somewhere. The store itself is extraordinary. The first two rooms are set into sandstone so that bedrock forms the floor and part of a back wall. Other rooms incorporate boulders sticking out from the stone and mud walls. Two particularly large specimens guard an outside door like a pair of carved lions; over one of these, a small window perches in imitation of a Cyclops eye. More than a home, it's an alliance with rock, a grand display of texture.

The post is also, a little sadly, for sale. The air around it seems dense, hushed, with the uneasiness of a beloved building awaiting its new owner. Carefully, my husband and I walk around the store, not too near, for our bodies are wary, afraid to intrude into a territory so strange and so clearly marked. In a rare gesture of authority, we make the children stay in the car.

"Could you live here?" my husband murmurs. I do not answer. After circling the post once, we stop at the For Sale sign and take down the number of the real estate agent. We will never call or, if we do, it will only be to satisfy a small curiosity. (How much, after all, do trading posts cost?) Yet it seems, at the time, an important piece of information. It is one of those byways. It is one of those things we hold in our pocket and finger because it gives us pleasure: a seashell design embedded in stone. As we leave, our tires spin in the gravel, and we take off in a familiar, gritty, romantic cloud of dust.

That would have been, I think, another life.

IRRIGATION

To own water, to control water, was the metaphor. Without water, the land is a corpse whispering soil into the wind, whispering enmities against the human race. *Sin agua no hay vida.* Without water, there is no life.

In 1981, when my husband and I moved to the Mimbres Valley, we eagerly went into debt for twelve acres transected by an irrigation ditch from which we have the right to water a one-acre field—enough water, exactly, to flood the acre yearly to the depth of 2.74 feet. This water is diverted from the Mimbres River by a dam upstream; we were, in essence, buying the river itself, buying snowpack on Reeds Peak, buying the rain. From the dam, two ditches—one on each side of the Mimbres—run three miles south and feed the fields of twenty irrigators. Plastered with concrete, these *acequias* are big enough for a four-year-old to both leap over or drown in during a fast flow. For one-half hour every eleven days, my husband and I have the right to open the tin gate inset in our part of the ditch and take the water as our own.

Under Western law, we were buying something as tangible and transferable as a sofa in a pickup truck. In more humid, eastern states, the riparian doctrine, inherited from the English, ensures landowners the use of water from any stream or river on their property. Landowners are also entitled not to have their stream flows retarded or diminished; the water—usually plentiful—is shared equally by all users. But in the marketplace of the West, this resource is too precious for such laissez faire. Most of the West follows the law of "prior appropriation," an idea derived in part from how early miners regulated what they needed to process gold. Here, the first man or woman who puts a stream to "beneficial use" has the first right to it in times of scarcity. Here, too, a water right is another property right, unconnected to the land. The right to irrigate, for example, from a stream or from the underground aquifer, can be sold to a farmer miles away in the same water basin. Or it can be leased to a nearby mine or city. (In the latter case, the amount of water that can be used legally also changes since different uses of water deplete the water system in different ways. In agriculture, as little as 30 percent of water seeps back to the aquifer. In a subdivision, 50 percent of water is returned as sewage effluent. Road construction takes nearly 100 percent of its withdrawal. And so on.)

Any transfer of a water right is highly regulated by the state engineer's office. It follows that the state engineer or "water czar" is one of the most politically powerful men in New Mexico. A simple business deal was when my neighbor leased his three-acre water right to a construction company repairing a highway bridge over the Mimbres River. The company got their water at a designated point downstream; instead of a garden that summer, my neighbor got a check. But when another farmer wanted to use acres and acres of his agricultural rights to pump water from the aquifer and pipe it to a nearby town, many people rushed personally to the state engineer's office. The rest of us telephoned. Would we be losing run-off normally returned to the Mimbres aquifer? Where exactly would this new well be located? How would it be metered? And who would do that?

There is, after all, only so much water in this valley. We all own chunks of it, and we are fiercely jealous owners.

While an irrigation right is considered commercial—a possible means of livelihood—a domestic water right is for private consumption only. In New Mexico, a homeowner applies for a domestic right when he or she drills a household well. That well can also be used in the Mimbres Valley to nurture a lawn, garden, or small orchard. In other water basins, such an outside "tap" or faucet might require the purchase of an additional water right. Domestic water comes from the ground below, pumped up with an electric motor or windmill, through a pipe that can be no larger than seven inches. It added to our sense of richness that on our land the previous owner had already drilled a well hitting the aquifer at eighty feet. Out of this, the water came up grandly, at twelve gallons a minute.

Looking out over our New World, like any new landowner, we wanted to literally hug the ground, to embrace it in our arms. The results would have been thorny. Yucca, buckhorn cholla, Apache plume, Emory oak, alligator juniper, desert bird-of-paradise, and mesquite dotted the grama grass above the concrete ditch. The field below the *acequia* bristled in weeds that amazed us with their elaborate and painful entrapments. In that field, we were constantly aware of the invisible water that washed back and forth: water that we owned, 2.74 feet a year! We watched the muddy rushing flow of the ditch. We counted up our annual fifteen inches of rain. We felt the very aquifer, that secret rocky womb, settle under our feet.

Land-poor. Water-wealthy. Our plan was to grow all our own food and save enormous amounts of money. Neither of us had ever gardened before although I had spent childhood summers on a Kansas farm. There I would pick flowers for my father's grave and pull onions which my grandmother sliced and ate raw between whole wheat bread. The memory of those onions lingered still, the dark soil clinging to fibrous roots, the miraculous whiteness when I peeled an outer layer of skin. I knew little more than this, and my lack of expectations had its advantage. Also because I had grown up in the urban Southwest, the complexity of irrigating my Mimbres land did not confound me. The fact that obtaining water was a matter of artifice and ingenuity and greed seemed perfectly normal.

In those first years we took the rules of irrigating very seriously. Our land was once part of the Gonzales ranch which receives a total of twelve hours every eleven days on the East San Lorenzo Community Ditch. This cycle of eleven days is based on how long alfalfa can survive without watering—a system less suitable for our little plot of vegetables and herbs. On the Gonzales ranch (as it is still named in the ditch schedule, some fifteen years after its development into a rural suburb) a one acre water right is worth a half-hour of time on the ditch. Confusingly, on other parts of the San Lorenzo Ditch, a one acre right might be worth twice that amount. In the nineteenth century, settlers bargained or simply took more minutes of water in exchange for maintaining the *acequia*. Such bargains hold fast today, in a system that mixes colonial Spanish custom with modern law.

The actual date of our half-hour varies with each irrigation cycle. Sometimes we watered on a pleasant Saturday afternoon. Sometimes it was Tuesday at two in the morning. If the water was high, all of us on the Gonzales ranch could open our gates at the same time, with plenty of flow for every field. If the water was low, my husband and I removed the lid that covered a hole in the concrete ditch, dammed the flow with a heavy piece of wood, and took all there was for a strict thirty minutes.

Even then, the rush of water could be daunting. Our part of the ditch is set well back on a bank above the field. In less than a second, its contents roared through a twenty-inch underground pipe to drop eight feet at the edge of our squash beds. A river was suddenly dashing against the tomato plants. A river was running through our land to the sea, whipped by the frenzy of gravity. At night in our beds, at the dinner table, or in casual conversation, all of us on the San Lorenzo Ditch dreamed of the perfect irrigation system. In this half-literary world—where mystical streams quickened to life chilies, trailing pumpkin, strawberries, and blue corn—the furrows would be sloped exactly right. The check dams would be efficient and permanent. The water would gallop in only to be carried off like a happy bride to every part of the field. There would be no waste, for the moment each plant had drunk its fill would be the moment to close the tin gate. High on the bank, a lazy god and goddess, my husband and I would look down over an earth heavy with fruit and flower.

In fact, as the flood burst onto the field, it traveled down a series of dirt furrows that often proved too steep, too shallow, too deep, too ephemeral. Soon parts of the garden looked like a rice paddy. Others required the work of a hoe to get a wayward trickle to each destined plant. Mud, more than water, was the truer element of our irrigation. Our boots grew heavy with it. Our shovels lifted and with gumbo slaps shaped the stuff into a hasty dam. Meanwhile, gopher holes siphoned the water into unpredictable places that required emergency patchworks of mud and rock. The gophers themselves popped up bewildered and wet-furred, and adrenaline ran high as my husband sprinted to kill them with his hoe. This was physical work, fast and furious, done often enough by the pink light of dawn, or the more eerie silver of the moon.

Ditch meetings were the other side of irrigating. In the past, a single large landholder had run the ditch and maintained it with his private crew and equipment. Some irrigators had long felt restless, and by the time we came rebellion was in the air. Voting on ditch matters was based on water rights, which gave our Anglo *patron,* who owned the most rights, an effective majority. Now, in a review of bylaws and state laws, the smaller landowners wanted to change to a one-man, one-vote system. This idea went to court and lost. Apparently, going to court was part of being on an irrigation ditch. At the first meeting I attended, one man had his lawyer with him. At that meeting, too, another couple sat outside in their truck rather than be in the same room with a certain neighbor. Such grudges—and there was more than one, there was talk of "filling the ditch with dead cows"—were usually the conflicts of old time ditch users, people who had had years to refine their animosities.

Despite all this—the gophers, the law suits—I thought of that time, when we were first irrigating, as halcyon. It was a time of innocence. We only saw the water then. We only saw our garden grow, never lush, never like Kansas, but full of bounty. In that time I learned about the sustanence of planting seeds. I saw my first corn come up, shoots of green sprouting from kernels, delicate whorls pushing through a hard crust. I saw wrinkled plant tissue becoming root, stalk, leaves; yellow flowers turning to heavy orbs; lime green pods opening like boats with their oarsmen of peas. All this skirted the edge of religion. For seconds, even moments in my garden, I understood that life was wonderful as well as terrible, that I was surrounded by powerful forces, that power shimmered in the air before me, that magic infiltrated the very ground.

With all my other "rights," tangled in the land and in the law, I have the right to walk the length of the East San Lorenzo Community Ditch. Ostensibly I am patroling for misuse or damage. Sometimes I go south past the border of the original Gonzales ranch, through Joe Garcia's land and Hortencia Thompkin's and on into the village of San Lorenzo itself. More often I head north up to the irrigation dam, walking on a rutted trail by fields of sweet-smelling alfalfa where the owners come out at sunset and throw firecrackers to scare off elk. When I reach the dam, I am, as usual, unimpressed. The ground is littered with the debris of broken branches and fence wire. The dam itself is two concrete basins where the Mimbres River is diverted to the west or east side of the San Lorenzo Ditch. Our ditch and its little dam is one of thirty-seven in the valley, with each ditch having from one to twenty members. Predictably, inter as well as intra ditch politics can be contentious.

Some years ago a member of the San Lorenzo Community Ditch went to court (again) to prove that our *acequia* was founded in 1869 and not 1870. Now, because we are officially the oldest, we have "first right" to the water in the Mimbres River. As the "senior appropriator," the San Lorenzo Community Ditch can take its full allotment—irrigating every field, every drop of my own 2.74 feet per acre per year—even if that means there is nothing left for junior ditches upstream and down. For the present, those ditches ignore this legality. In our second year of drought, one man upstream simplifies irrigation by bulldozing his own dam across the river and turning it onto his field. Gun shots have been fired for less. When the Mimbres Valley is finally adjudicated (a legal process in which all existing water rights are confirmed) or when the noose of drought tightens around all our necks, then the finer points of water law may be enforced—first by the *mayordomo,* a man or woman hired on each ditch to play the role of cop, and next by the state engineer's department, the sheriff, the highway patrol, the state police, etc. Then, as one of our ditch commissioners says, we'll really be living in the wild West.

For the moment, our ditch has three commissioners, but no *mayordomo.* The temptation to steal water is great, and just about every irrigator in the valley succumbs. Flamboyantly they bull-doze the river or, more sneakily, leave their gate askew so that a constant flow trickles to some favorite strawberry patch. They lease their rights to a mining company and continue to use the water. They take an extra hour or an extra day. We do it our-selves. We have a sneaky trickle to a planting of young cotton-woods. Just as we have learned about the complexity, the sheer messiness of irrigating our land, so we now see the tension and litigious fever raging below the valley's pretty pastoral scene.

In the larger picture of the West, conflicts over water have also escalated. When the Texan city of El Paso asked for permits to drill in southern New Mexico, a court battle began that farmers viewed as the approximation of war. "El Paso wants to keep us like a colony," said one bitter agriculturalist. "We're a poor state, let's face it, and they want us to stay that way." Other cities like Denver and Tucson are also going to court with their rural neigh-bors; Los Angeles has squared off with northern California, Mex-ico with the United States.

There are few heros in this war. Certainly the farmer does not qualify. In New Mexico, irrigated agriculture already takes 90 percent of the state's water, consumes it the most (meaning that the water is evaporated, transpired by plants, or lost to the ocean or some unusuable aquifer), and probably wastes it the most. Some of the waste can be blamed on another Western water law: "Use it or lose it." If my husband and I do not water our field for four years, we could forfeit the right to do so. Thus in years that we do not have a garden, it is to our advantage to flood the field anyway in the gratuitous production of something. Environ-mentalists in the Southwest have the added burden of proving

that leaving water in a stream—for deer, say, or fish or beaver—
is using it. Traditionally, diverting water has been the only way
to establish and keep a water right.

Most dramatically, inefficient irrigation has been encouraged
by the federal subsidization of massive dams and engineering
projects. For such a scarce resource, water is provided astonish-
ingly cheap to Western farmers. On my own ditch, in my own
little world, we are trying to replace our aging concrete *acequia*
with a pipeline. The entire project would cost about one hundred
thousand dollars of which federal and state funds, if available,
could pay as much as 85 percent. My share would be about fifty
dollars. With their costs so subsidized, large-scale farmers often
have no incentive to conserve.

Today nearly all Western rivers have been dammed and mul-
tiply dammed, and some Western aquifers are in danger of de-
pletion. One end product is that irrigation accounts for 12
percent of American crop land. Another result is that agricultural
lifestyles have been maintained in the arid West. There is argument now as to whether the results are worth the cost. There is,
as my husband and I have discovered, a new layer of contention
to peel.

Conflict takes on another dimension when it is between races.
One reason my husband and I chose to move to southern rather
than northern New Mexico is that racial tensions here are not as
high. Northern communities like Espanola and Taos were His-

panic strongholds hundreds of years ago, and they continue to skirmish with the Indians who were there before them as well as the Anglos who came after. In the Mimbres Valley, copper was discovered by the Spanish around 1804, but in the first half of the nineteenth century, Apaches prevented any real farming. In 1848, America won a war with Mexico and took this part of their country as booty. A decade later, the American army began to establish forts, and the local Apaches were "pacified" to the extent that none remain here today. Finally, in the late 1860s and 1870s, both Anglos and Hispanics could seriously work the land, at about the same time, and with equal claims to it.

This does not mean that the dominant Anglo culture did not dominate, or that Hispanics did not resent the Anglo presence. Older people can still remember the years, in the 1950s, when public bathrooms and swimming pools were segregated, when Hispanic miners were paid less, and Hispanics were denied that cherished American right—upward mobility. Today, most of that has changed for the better, and the two races, particularly in city and county government, seem equally represented. What has not changed is a strong sense of separatism: bi-cultural, bi-lingual, not a melting pot. This describes most of New Mexico, a state in which Anglos, Hispanics, and Native Americans never cared to assimilate each other. In my valley, at least, Anglos and Hispanics live side by side, in varying degrees of hostility and friendship, in a mutual acceptance of boundaries and differences and of their importance.

Recently, such separatism has sharpened on the San Lorenzo Community Ditch.

"There has always been a problem," says one of my Anglo neighbors. He has stopped me on the road, so that we are talking through a car window. "And people, on both sides, have always tried to move beyond it. Lately, we've regressed. Last year at the ditch cleanup, we all worked as a team. We came and cleared out the ditch and shared a beer afterwards. This year, the Hispanics came together, moved off on their own, and left on their own."

My neighbor is concerned and discouraged. But I suspect this regression to be the shadow of a more positive activism. The **Asociacion de Acequias del Valle Rio Mimbres** is a group recently formed here under the wing of a larger New Mexico Acequia Association. Composed of three officers (all from the San Lorenzo Community Ditch) with eight potential members "interested but cautious," at first the local meetings were for Hispanics only. Later the group recanted and are now open to any *parciante* or irrigator in the valley. Their priority is to oversee the coming adjudication of the Mimbres and to make sure that the larger, predominantly Anglo landowners do not use the legal system unfairly. Their interest in this is personal: at least one officer has a quarrel with a specific Anglo landowner.

A larger goal of the **Asociacion** is to promote a state arbitration board where complaints on *acequias* can be heard without going through a costly court case. More ambitious still, they would like to reform the water laws. They are against the separation of a water right from the land itself. They are against policies which consider only the highest economic good and smooth the transfer of water traditionally used by small Hispanic and

Native American farmers. They are for the support of agriculture as an expression of culture. They are, in their minds, trying to divert some of the run-off in New Mexico's favorite cliche: water flows uphill to money.

Politically, the young president of the **Asociacion de Acequias del Valle Rio Mimbres** and I have much in common. We share suspicions about progress and American technology. We both romanticize the agricultural lifestyle. We live in houses that value the textures of mud and wood. He admits that most Hispanic men and women have rejected farming for better paying jobs at the mines or for professional careers. They ignore or neglect their inherited plots of irrigated land. He admits that no one can make a living off these plots. Still, like me, he sees the power of growing food. He is proud that his own bottom field yielded four hundred pounds of beans last year. He fantasizes about the destruction of our over-complex, high-tech society. Maybe there will be a depression. A war! Only those on the land will be safe, he says. Deeply, irrationally, I agree. "If we have the water," he tells me, "we won't go hungry."

In other ways, this man and I will never be friends. In other ways he makes me feel excluded, as a woman, as a white woman. This is his right, and I do not take it to heart. Segregation is a social reality. But it is not always enough to affect the real life of people. Recently, when I visited an older friend of mine, she mourned and fretted over the marriage of her Hispanic daughter to an Anglo man. She did it in front of me as she pieced together a gift, a quilt for my own daughter. She did it because, for the moment, she had forgotten that I am an Anglo too. That's the way it is with a friend; you sometimes forget that she or he is not you.

In the metaphor of owning water, fruit trees play an important role. Fruit trees indicate a long-range plan. They are a link to the future. And they are sweet, fulfilling that primal need for asorbic acid and fast-energy fructose, for hedonism and a harvest of dessert.

In the story of our orchard (and all orchards have stories), my husband struck something hard and strange three feet down while digging a hole for the seventh tree. It wasn't a big rock. It was a series of rocks, made into a wall, turning a corner, and proceeding again. At the second corner we found a jagged piece of charcoal. For a while, we abandoned fruit trees in favor of excavation. A thousand years ago the Mimbreno Indians planted tepary beans here, Gila squash, and varieties of corn. The buried homes of the Indians are scattered throughout the valley, and now we hoped that these underground walls were an actual Mimbreno site, a room still inhabited by memories and pots.

If so, it wasn't a very good site, right on the river bottom. When an amateur archeologist dropped by—a profession held by many in the Mimbres Valley—she shook her head doubtfully over the holes. She suggested that this was, instead, an irrigation system, perhaps from the Mimbrenos, or perhaps from farmers only a hundred years dead. The latter seemed more probable after we began to uncover broken bits of blue and white porcelein. By this time our field looked ravaged, and the fruit trees were wilting in their nursery containers. Abashed, we filled in the trenches and planted a Bartlett above the stone walls.

That was three years ago, and that was the last thing we ever planted in the field. I was pregnant with our second child and in the fall, harvest time, after the baby was born, I would resume teaching. My husband had started working as an outfitter, and fall was the time he took his clients into the woods. Fall, in fact, had always been our nemesis. Pickling, canning, baking, chopping, grinding, blanching, freezing: I associated these things with masochism and an unhealthy indoor sweat. The fruit trees were our last burst of energy. That very spring, cold turkey, we ended our love affair with the field, our precious irrigated land. We put away the ditch schedule, watched the weeds take over, watered the fruit trees irregularly and then, as the seasons passed, watered them less and less.

What we lost in those years was more than fresh vegetables. We lost, unknowingly, a relationship to the community. We stopped seeing certain friends because we no longer needed to see them about the ditch. We stopped going to the annual ditch cleanup (a subtext of my neighbor's conversation through the car window) and so didn't hear about the latest grandchild or the man's daughter who had died of leukemia. A rancher upstream cheated gloriously, water flooding onto his fields, and we didn't care. The drought of 1990 worsened, the ditch ran dry in June, and we didn't care either. I personally lost people—large ruddy men who chewed tobacco, Hispanic housewives, teenagers aching to be rodeo stars—with whom I had little in common but with whom I could engage, honestly, when it came to talking water. I lost a handful of conversations. I lost that sense of skipping over differences to land in the middle of some ancient, coordinated, physical ritual where we watered the land together and heard it give thanks.

Without that ritual, my connection to the land and to the metaphor that brought us here has begun to fade. At the same time, I see more clearly what the metaphor meant to us and what we wanted when we bought irrigated land.

We wanted, certainly, a sense of independence. We wanted adulthood and the self-sufficiency of feeding ourselves. Naively, we wanted freedom from the exigency of earning money. We had no idea how underpriced food is or how small a part the "savings" in potatoes and chilies would play in our budget. We vastly underestimated our preference for processed food, wine, Diet-Cokes, and Fritos. We overestimated our ability to transform ourselves, to become more primitive, more sensual, thinner, browner, healthier. We wanted purity: to raise pure children, to eat soil and sun. I wanted, I see now, the safety I saw in my Kansas grandmother, that woman who survived the Depression and loss of her youngest child, who lived fully and cheerfully into her nineties. I wanted a charm against my fear of catastrophe, my fear that society would let me down. To paraphrase: "As long as I have water, I will never become a bag lady."

Transformation, safty, serenity. I am not yet convinced that a plot of irrigated land will not bring me these things. That is why I have continued to collect seed catalogs and why this spring I have put them all together into a big pile. I am planning a garden, the first in three years, and the biggest ever. I can close my eyes and see it: Triumph de Farcy and Kentucky Wonder pole; Kinko carrots and Scarlet Nantes; shiny, waxy, elegant eggplant; rows of military Spanish onions; jalapenos, serranos, sandias, chile piquin; Jersey Golden Acorn and Cocozelle squash; gorgeous tomatoes; ferny asparagus; exotic tomatillos; beds of lettuce—Oakleaf, Ruby Red, Kagran Summer.

I am planning a new irrigation system, a perfect one with little dams that I will hammer myself out of wood and tin, with furrows calculated to just the right incline, with a mystical stream quickening to life my chilies and blue corn.

I am even planning the fall harvest. I will quit my teaching job and build a pantry. I will learn to love canning and my house will overflow with jars: amber, sea green, maroon, yellow-orange. I will have so many that I must give half of them away. Each jar will be another form of water. Water turned to food. Water turned to neighbors. Water turned to children. Water turned to me.

GILA WILDERNESS

Perched high on their horses, completely unafraid, the children are pretending to be English tourists.

"I say, look at that over there, old boy!"

"Old boy, old boy. Look at that!" Maria repeats gleefully. She is not quite five and Eric is seven. They have squabbled off and on all morning over who would ride in front and then who would ride in back and then who would ride in front again. Eric's mother, Lana, is leading the horse, in part because I am nervous when we walk downhill and the big animal crowds behind me. I wonder where these children have picked up the nuances of satire and funny accents. Videos, I suppose. TV. Their ideas, to be sure, are still vague. When we ask Eric where England is, he looks shifty and then says with authority, "In Pennsylvania."

There is plenty of time to talk on this five mile hike and family pack train. My son, nearly two, is fulfilling a dream he has held half his life, for he, too, is high on a horse, his excitement contained by Lana's ten-year-old daughter, his horse led by Lana's husband. At the back, my husband leads two more horses packed with camping gear. At the front, Roberta and her married daughter Carol Greene walk the trail. Carol has left behind her family in Wisconsin to be with her mother now, and while I am freshly creating my children's memories, Carol and Roberta are sorting through their own. A little high in protest, Carol's voice can be heard as they ascend a hill. Roberta's answer is carried away by the wind.

Although I have lived here for eight years—although I can see from the ridge above my home the green edge of the Gila National Forest—the next four days will be my longest trip into the Gila Wilderness, my fourth trip only, the one in which I will best comprehend wilderness, and the one in which I will start scheming, immediately after, as to how I can return.

It's ironic. Like most people, I associate wilderness with being alone. The 1964 National Wilderness Act, which legislated our country's system of wildernesses, is specific about this and includes "outstanding opportunities for solitude" as part of its definition of what a wilderness is. Historically, bred deep in our cultural bones, we think of the solitary explorer and hunter: men with righteous-sounding names like Daniel Boone or Jedediah Smith. Socially, we believe that the point of wilderness is to get away from people. Spiritually, we want to meet Nature stripped of our accoutrements and modern "superficial" selves. We want to be that vulnerable. We want to be that arrogant—the only human being on earth!

Yet here I am, with four children, five adults, and four horses. My husband and Lana's husband are partners in a new outfitting company, and they have condescended to treat their families to what they provide paying customers. Thus we are well-equipped, with therma-rest pads, big tents, and down sleeping bags. We have disposable diapers and storybooks and sunscreen lotion. We have pork tenderloin for tonight's dinner, fresh asparagus, wine glasses, and a cheesecake. As a mother and wife and friend, I have all my usual concerns. We have, I think, left only the dogs, the cats, and the videos behind.

Our trail runs through dry rolling hills dotted with juniper, scrub oak, and pinon pine. There are three colors: the parched yellow of grama grass, the dark of evergreen trees, the pale blue sky. This is peaceful country, and if its vistas are not grand, they call, nonetheless, to those parts of the body which have always yearned to fly. Sometimes the trail crosses an outcropping of bleak rhyolite or a bed of pink, eroded stone. Sometimes we swing around the side of a hill, and Lana's daughter gets nervous, unsure of her horse's footing on the narrow path.

"Davy, Davy, horsie, Davy," she comforts herself by crooning to my son. Ahead of her, Eric and Maria are much alike; three-quarters in an interior world, they squeal so hilariously that Lana, whom I admire for her patience, must tell them to be quiet.

We all stop to watch a red-tailed hawk.

Then we began our descent, down Little Bear Canyon to the Middle Fork of the Gila River.

For my husband, this loss of altitude is a psychic passage. Rather quickly, the canyon begins to narrow and the sky shuts down until it is a swatch of blue in a pattern of pine boughs and fir needles. In a world grown suddenly cool, we are walking on the stream bed with its trickling flow and ledges of rock that rise above us. A grassy bench shelters a stand of yellow columbine; we stop again while the girls exclaim and wax sentimental. All around us, in contrast to the hills above, the murmuring life has been nurtured by water. Insects hatch and burrow in the mud. Emerald green algae swirls in a puddle. The canyon deepens and the rock rises above us, so close we could almost extend our arms and touch each wall. Now there is only rock and water and we are moving darkly to the center of the earth.

Then, like the odd turn in a dream, the stream bed expands to the size of a living room. Above is a small cave which my husband announces as a prehistoric shrine. The children are lifted down from their horses; the older ones scramble up the rock face. My husband tells us that not long ago you could still find prayer sticks and arrowheads here, scattered on the ground. These artifacts were from the Mogollon Culture: weavers, potters, basketmakers, and farmers who by A.D. 900 had upgraded their pithouses into multi-room villages of stone and mud. Slighter and shorter than we are today, the Mogollons had a life expectancy of forty-five years and babies who died rather frequently. At this site, they have left a few faded pictographs—a squiggle I might generously call a lizard, a red hand that is oddly evocative. Carefully, Lana's daughter puts her own hand over the ancient print, covering it completely.

We emerge from Little Bear Canyon, as my husband said we would, into the light. Streaming down from the center of the sky, reflected in the water and trembling cottonwood leaves, bouncing up from banks of white sand, the sun seems to explode around us. It is a drought year, and the Middle Fork of the Gila is not as large as usual. Still, it looks grandly like a river, with riffles and pools and a fiery gleam that disappears around corners left and right. High over the water, red cliffs form the towers of an abandoned city, with tapered ends eroded into strange balancing acts. Here the riparian ecology includes walnut, sycamore, cottonwood, willow, wild grape, and Virginia creeper. Herons and kingfishers hunt the shallows. Trout rise for bugs. These sudden shifts in environment, accomplished in a few hours of walking, are not unusual in the Gila Wilderness. On some day trips, a hiker can move from the Chihuahuan desert to a Subalpine forest. Diversity is the rule, with five life zones and a thousand microclimates, all determined by water or its lack.

Water is our goal as well, and the mothers take the children to the river, letting the men deal with horses and lunch. Maria joins Lana's daughter, who is busy making dams and catching tadpoles. Eric attempts to disappear forever, but Lana knows him well and is prepared for this. She hauls him from the underbrush and informs him firmly: he is only seven, he can not leave her yet. My own son picks up a stick and begins to splash me. Then, who knows why, he is suddenly anxious and wants only to nurse.

A half mile from our planned campsite, we eat in a small grove of ponderosa pine. When it is time to pack up, Maria wants to sit in front on the horse again. It's not your turn, we tell her, it's Eric's turn. Maria has a tantrum. Six parents stand around, cajoling a little, making deals. She can ride in front later; we'll tell her a story. She accepts the good part—she'd love a story—but rejects the bad. Finally, my husband takes a stand. Maria can not ride unless she rides in back.

So I am left amid the ponderosa pine with my screaming child. Ponderosa are beautiful trees. Unlike other local conifers, their long needles extend out and away, giving this pine an oriental delicacy. In many parts of the Gila, ponderosa form vast, parklike forests where the trees rise a hundred feet, the crowns do not touch, and the accumulated needles make a deep carpet free of undergrowth. These are, as well, trees with a secret: breathe deep into their reddish bark and you are suffused with the faint scent of vanilla.

I try to show this to Maria as she cries fiercely, piercingly. I hug her, in a physical effort to contain an emotion of which she has clearly become the victim. Following one school of thought, for a while I simply let her express the emotion. I wait and admire the beautiful trees. My patience for waiting is not long, but in that time I am surprisingly content. This is my job, I think. Socialization. Taking turns. I am grateful for where I am. In a public place, or even a friend's home, I could not endure this blast of feeling.

"Maria," I say, like a fisherman baiting a hook, knowing well she will succumb, "I'll tell you a story while we walk."

The storm subsides slowly; Maria is beached on shore, looking bewildered. Where has she been? We hold hands and follow the trail along the riverbank, through shady groves and then out, once more, into the sun. I tell her about Hansel and Gretel, and when we reach the campsite, everyone is happy to see us. The camp itself is full of miraculous signs. In a pool, deep enough for bathing, a group of fish sway in the shadows. Nearby, three baby birds with wide mouths complain from their nest. A swallowtail butterfly circles the stalk of a purple bull thistle. Two trees for a hammock stand perfectly apart.

As we go about the business of setting up camp, our son opens and empties a bottle of brandy on our clothes. In the rustles inside newly erected tents, I know that other family dramas are going on, and I am beginning to see that older children bring a whole new set of interesting problems. Roberta is hurt by something Carol has said. Lana's daughter is unhappy about the dinner arrangements. Lana is trying to keep Eric from under the horses' feet.

The horses themselves are engaged in complex social arrangements. I had never known that they could be so human, so insistent in their desires. One horse doesn't like the other and won't be picketed beside her. Two of the horses are set free to graze because my husband knows they are too loyal to leave while their partners are tied up. Much later, in the middle of the night, the mare begins to scream with jealousy and rage: another horse has broken loose and is eating grass. This she can not abide.

The afternoon slips away with the sounds of children playing in the river. Around the evening campfire I shelter my son just as these green cottonwoods shelter us. Lana's husband also holds his ten-year-old daughter, the girl's long legs crowding her father's lap. Roberta and Carol are thoughtfully quiet while Maria and Eric can be heard from a tent, whispering secrets.

We are not the first family group to laze under these trees and count our riches and our sorrows. In a wilderness, relatively few humans have come before and it is permissible, I think, to imagine an intersection. I imagine an Indian family, descendents of

Asians who crossed the Bering Strait and came to this area after the Mogollons and before the Spanish. The Zunis christened these nomads Apache—the word for enemy. I imagine wicki-ups instead of tents, pine boughs for softness, hides for warmth, *metates, manos,* beads from Mexico.

"In that country which lies around the headwaters of the Gila I was reared," dictated Geronimo when he was old, exiled, and still homesick. "This range was our fatherland; among these mountains our wigwams were hidden; the scattered valleys contained our fields; the boundless prairies, stretching away on every side, were our pastures; the rocky caverns were our burying places. I was fourth in a family of eight children—four boys and four girls. . . . I rolled on the dirt floor of my father's teepee, hung in my cradle at my mother's back, or slept suspended from the bough of a tree. I was warmed by the sun, rocked by the winds, and sheltered as other Indian babes."

As a boy growing up in these forests and mountains, Geronimo's life would have been greatly envied by Lana's son. In the Apache's words, he "played at hide and seek among the rocks and pines" or "loitered in the shade of the cottonwood trees" or worked with his parents in the cornfields. Sometimes, to avoid the latter, he and his friends would sneak out of camp and hide all day in some secret dappled meadow or sunny canyon. If caught, they were subject to ridicule. If not, they could expect to return at twilight, victorious and unpunished. Geronimo's father died when he was small and at seventeen years of age—1846, the year the United States declared war on Mexico—the teenager was admitted into the tribe's council of warriors. Soon after, the young man married his version of a high school sweetheart and together they had three children. This first wife, Alope, was artistic. To beautify their home amid the vanilla-scented pine, she made decorations of beads and drew pictures on buckskin.

Later, as Geronimo tells it, he and his tribe went to Mexico to trade. There Mexican troops attacked the camp while the men were in town. Geronimo's mother, wife, and three children were killed. Stunned, the warrior vowed vengeance and went on to fight both Mexicans and Americans in a guerrilla warfare that was mean and dirty by all accounts and on all sides. "Even babies were killed," one Apache warrior regretted later. "And I love babies!"

Here in the Gila headwaters, local chiefs had long fought the parade of settlers and prospectors. The end was inevitable. In 1886, Geronimo, the last holdout, surrendered and was shipped to Florida along with every other Indian who had ever made the Gila a home. Even the Apache scouts who had helped bring Geronimo in were loaded onto the boxcars. In the 1890s a newspaper reported with nostalgia and some compassion that a "wild and half-starved" Apache family had been seen foraging in the rugged Mogollon Mountains. Desperate and surely lonely, they died or left by the end of the century.

In the morning, my husband gets up early and walks with David and Maria to the nearby hot springs. I follow later and for half an hour, I am, in fact, solitary in the wilderness.

Self-consciously, I look about the scene of a fast-flowing river, lined with leafy trees, against a background of rock. It is conventionally pretty. It is also hard edged and muscular, Southwestern tough. I have the strong feeling that I am not the dominant species here.

This, too, is an echo of the 1964 Wilderness Act, which declares that "a wilderness, in contrast with those areas where man and his own works dominate the landscape, is hereby recognized as a place where the earth and its community of life are untrammeled by man, where man is a visitor who does not remain."

Frankly, I like this lack of power and control. I like being a visitor. Here in the wilderness I can put aside my grievances against humanity. I can exchange, at the very least, one set of complexities for another: the dappled slant of a bank, rustling leaves, straight white trunks, crumbling cliff faces, gravel slopes, turbulent water—all glowing with sunlight, intertwined, patterned; rich with diatoms, moss, algae, caddisflies, dragonflies, damselflies, stoneflies, trout, suckers, bass, minnows, chubs; pinchers, mouthparts, claws, teeth; photosynthesis, decomposition, carbonization. None of it is my doing. I am just a large mammal walking the riverbank. Ahead is my mate.

When I was fifteen, I lied to my mother and hitchhiked from my home in Phoenix to camp out in a sycamore-lined canyon above the desert. The point was to do this alone. The point was to be alone and serene and in touch with beauty. The trip, unsurprisingly for a girl raised in the suburbs, was a disaster, and I ended up leaving a day early. On the way home, the old man who gave me a ride tried once to put his hand on my thigh. The image lingered with me for many years. The stubby white fingers. My revulsion. My ignorance.

When I was eighteen, a girlfriend and I planned a summer-long backpack trip that would take us four hundred miles up the Pacific Crest Trail. The girlfriend dropped out at the last minute, and I went on by myself, determined this time to live alone in the woods. Outside Ashland, Oregon, I watched the dawn beneath layers of a plastic tarp against which mosquitos hammered and whined for my blood. At that time I was still concerned about my alienation from nature, and I perceived a sheet of glass, a terrible wall, between me and life, me and experience. For days, I hiked through a pine forest that never seemed to vary or end, until my thoughts too began to hammer and whine at the bone of my skull. One evening I cried after swimming in a lake and finding my body, my legs and crotch, covered with small red worms. A week later I met a boy my age who was also alone, and we traveled together the rest of the summer, hitchhiking north to mountains that began where timberline ended. We never grew to like each other. We never had the slightest physical contact. Yet we hung on, gamely, blindly, to the comfort and distraction of another human being.

When I was twenty, I set out again, this time bicycling with a college classmate up the East Coast. She ended her tour in Maine, and the next day I started for Nova Scotia. By now I knew what it meant to travel alone as a female: I knew about circumspection, reserve, hiding. In Canada, the ocean exploded against a lushness of farmland, and for me this was exotic, stupendous surrealism. I tried my best to internalize the scenery. But it seemed that I could only turn wheels, pushing my limit, sixty miles up and down the green hills, a hundred miles on the flat inland highway between the tips of the island. By now I knew as well when to recognize misery, and in Halifax I prepared to pack up and head back to school. Instead—a postscript—I met another bicyclist, fell in love with him, and stayed on through a long winter.

Somewhere in all that, I gave up on my ability to conquer solitude. I had tried to be my version of Daniel Boone, brave and self-sufficient, to seek distance and the lonely sound of foreign names. My model could have come straight from the Gila Wilderness. I had tried to be—not Geronimo, who was too much the warrior—but such a man as James Ohio Pattie, a twenty-year-old who trapped beaver on the Gila River five years before Geronimo was ever born. By his own account, Pattie left Missouri in 1824, traveled to Santa Fe where he rescued the governor's daughter from Commanches, managed the copper mines in Santa Rita, escaped massacre by Pimas in Arizona, floated the Colorado River to its salty mouth, starved in a Spanish jail, and crossed Mexico to sell his memoirs to a publisher in St. Louis.

In this case, as I walk beside the Middle Fork, it is not fanciful to imagine that I am following Pattie's footsteps. In his narrative of the 1824 trip, he clearly reaches the hot springs where we will picnic this afternoon. Typically, his description is more dramatic than seems reasonable. He writes of catching a fish and throwing it in the spring's boiling waters where "in six minutes it would be thoroughly cooked." Other tales are equally elongated, and it has become a historian's game to match up Pattie's journey with the rest of history. His account of daily dangers are the most credible: the terror of meeting a grizzly bear or the hunger that forced him and his partners to shoot their dogs. On one sad day, Pattie wrote piteously, "We killed a raven, which we cooked for seven men." By the end of his adventures, he had probably become what he most admired—the quintessential mountain man. Still, it is a lesson to me that James Ohio Pattie, living out the romance, felt so strongly the need to romanticize. For at that time the governor had no daughter, it was another trapper who fought the Pimas, and another man who killed the grizzly.

In 1924, a hundred years after Pattie explored the Middle Fork, three-quarter million acres of the Gila National Forest were designated by the Forest Service as "an area big enough to absorb a two weeks' pack trip and kept devoid of roads, artificial trails, cottages, or other works of man." This was the first official wilderness in the United States, the beginning of our national wilderness system, and the brainchild of a thirty-seven-year-old forester named Aldo Leopold. In my own history, upon returning from Nova Scotia and my first, unsuccessful love affair—upon giving up the idea of becoming a mountain man—I settled instead on becoming Aldo Leopold. I read his famous work *Sand County Almanac* and I changed my college major from drama to natural resources. I took courses in wildlife management, the field that Leopold pioneered, and wrote papers on deer herd reduction. I even took a course from Leopold's son, Starker Leopold, whom I glamorized on the slightest of proofs. My hero became not the man who lives wilderness, but the one who manages it.

Years later, when I came to live near the Gila Wilderness, my attachment to Leopold increased for an odd reason. I learned more about his mistakes. They were not small. After a boyhood beside the Mississippi River, Aldo Leopold went East to the Yale Forestry School and then Southwest as a greenhorn foreman of a timber crew. At first, this sportsman thought mainly in terms of hunting and fishing. He had no problems with grazing either and eventually had friends and relatives at both of the big ranches in the Gila Forest. With these connections, and in his later role as a game and fish manager, Leopold pushed hard for predator control and vowed to extinguish every killer of deer and cow, "down to the last wolf and lion."

In the Gila area, he hired hunter extraordinaire Ben Lilly, who by 1921 had a lifetime lion kill of five hundred. Today there is a Ben Lilly Monument in the Gila National Forest with a plaque dedicated to the memory of a man who shot more wildlife in the Southwest than anyone else would ever want to. With all his outdoor expertise, Ben Lilly is not a man I would want my children to emulate. Violence was his tie to nature. And when his dogs "betrayed their species" by being poor hunters, he beat them to death.

In the late 1920s an irruption of deer in the Gila and nearby Black Range caused Aldo Leopold to rethink his ideas on predator control. Twenty years after the fact he describes shooting at a wolf and her half-grown cubs from a high rimrock. In seconds, the mother and children were dead or scattered. Leopold rushed down in time to catch a "fierce green fire" dying in the old wolf's eyes.

"I thought that because fewer wolves meant more deer, no wolves would mean a hunter's paradise," the conservationist wrote in his essay "Thinking Like a Mountain." "But after seeing the green fire die, I sensed that neither the wolf nor the mountain agreed with such a view. Since then I have lived to see state after state extirpate its wolves. I have watched the face of many a newly wolfless mountain, and seen the south-facing slopes wrinkle with a maze of new deer trails. I have seen every edible bush and seedling browsed, first to anaemic desuetude, and then to death . . . In the end the starved bones of the hoped-for deer herd, dead of its own too much, bleach with the bones of the dead sage, or molder under the high-lined junipers. I now suspect that just as a deer herd lives in mortal fear of its wolves, so does a mountain live in mortal fear of its deer."

By the time Leopold himself died, in 1949, he saw wilderness in a much richer light than the one that prompted him, in 1924, to push for a "national hunting ground" in the Gila Forest. Wilderness areas were still important as sanctuaries for the primitive arts of canoeing, packing, and hunting. But they were also necessary as part of a larger land ethic and as a laboratory for the study of land health. Culturally, wilderness was a place where Americans could rediscover their history and "organize yet another search for a durable scale of values." Wilderness even had something that Leopold could not name. "The physics of beauty," he noted, "is one department of natural science still in the Dark Ages."

It is, perhaps, not surprising that as the country's first wilderness, the Gila may also be the most mismanaged. In part due to its bloated deer herds, in the late 1920s a road was opened through the heart of the wilderness to allow access to hunters. Another road to the Gila Cliff Dwellings National Monument would later be paved. In 1964, historic grazing leases were granted "in perpetuity," and along certain streams cattle have clearly become the dominant species. The imperfections of the Gila carry their own lessons. To become a visitor, to relinquish control, is not easy.

When I reach the hot springs, I have reached a place like my husband's passage through Little Bear Canyon, a place that conforms to a place inside. Surrounded by ferns and vegetation, the two pools are sheltered against a massive rock upon which the hot water trickles down in a cascade over slick moss and lime green algae. A hand built dam of loose stone creates a four-foot-deep swimming hole in which the older children play and splash. The water temperature is about a hundred degrees. My husband stretches full length and lets his nose touch the tiny yellow wildflowers that bloom at the pool's edge.

I carry my son David against my chest. He is developing his sense of humor and, to amuse him, I simulate disgust when he sticks out his tongue so that it fills his little mouth. "Oooooh!" I make a face. He laughs with power and sticks out his tongue again. "Ooooh!" I say. He grins and sticks out his tongue at everyone. All the girls, excepting his sister, want to hold him in their arms and glide away with him in the warm water. He skims over the surface of the pool and then cries out so beseechingly that they float him back to me. Clinging, he rides my hip like a cowboy in the saddle. We go through cycles with our children, as they do with us, and for now my son, who is twenty-two months, and I, who am thirty-five years, are besotted with each other. I adore his skin and his smell and every stray expression that informs his face with intelligence and personality. This is mutual, unconditional love—an exotic interlude. This has been going on in these hot springs since the first Mogollon mother, since Alope and her children.

The rest of the trip passes in this way. We take turns riding the horses farther up the Middle Fork: here the rock walls loom a thousand feet above a canyon floor that narrows dramatically to the width of its river. Another few miles and the trail runs down-hill, faster and faster, as the horses hurry to a grassy bottom land known as The Meadows. The scenery is breathtaking and we claim it as our own. No one has ever seen it, just this way, before. In the cooling twilights, we swim in the water hole. During an afternoon rain, we lie in our tents. We cook. We talk. We clean. Roberta and Carol take long walks together. Spouses, as usual, spar a little, and the children bicker. On our therma-rest pads, we all sleep well.

Later, driving home, I have to wonder why these four days

have been such a success. Who was it—my husband, my children, my friends—who helped me to see, just a little more clearly, that I do not need to become more than I am to have a place in the wilderness? I do not need to love solitude more than the company of my own species. I do not need to become a man. Or a manager. The shrine is here already. The graves. The bowls and the baskets and the way we touch a baby or tell stories to children. I need only walk in.

RANGE WAR

T he room is full of ranchers. The young ones look traditionally lean, while on the older men the tight-fitting Western
shirt and jeans mercilessly reveal every sign of aging, from the
slumped shoulder to the hanging belly. Everyone in the room is
deeply tanned. Many are angry. They sit on metal folding chairs,
arms across their chests, not bending to chat with a neighbor or
friend, but waiting silently for the meeting to begin. As I sign
the register, a bullish-looking man also waits for me to identify
myself, to write under the appropriate space Silver City *Daily
Press* or Diamond D Bar or Audubon Society. He stares at me
intently. I leave that part blank.

This meeting is for us, the public, to express our views to a
task force of ten men ranged in a semicircle at the front of the
room. What draws us here is the growing competition between
elk and livestock in the Gila National Forest. Exterminated in
the 1900s, reintroduced elk can now be seen in herds of fifty to
two hundred, their big angular bodies flashing across a meadow
or retreating ghostlike into the shadows of pine. Goaded by a
recent drought, these herds are coming down from the high
mountains to eat on pastures where ranchers who lease the public
lands traditionally graze cows. By the end of this meeting, one

rancher will be pounding the table in front of him, shouting "All we get is the runaround! There are people going broke here!" At the same time, today marks the end of a hunt in which twenty elk, most of them pregnant, were legally killed out of season. The untimely death of these animals did not please local hunters and outfitters. Environmentalists, too, are asking the question they believe is rhetorical: who has first right on our wilderness areas and national forests? Meanwhile, land shared by cattle and elk is becoming daily, perhaps seriously, overgrazed.

It is the Forest Service who organized this task group and this meeting. They have hired a facilitating firm to field questions and summarize our statements onto big sheets of paper which are taped up hurriedly all over the room. At first I am amused by these New Age professionals: a studiously friendly man in slacks and loose shirt and a well-dressed woman assistant. Rather soon, I see how necessary they are. The comments begin with direct, undisguised hostility. The ranchers feel that both the Forest Service and the Game and Fish Department should have prevented the increase in elk and are not doing enough about the problem now.

"It's one lousy job of management," a man scolds the District Range and Wildlife Supervisor. "If we manage cows, we should be managing wildlife!"

"In 1905, 1906, we made an agreement with you guys," an elderly man, whose painful body movements speak of a life falling off horses and getting back on, uses his wife's arm for support as he speaks. "The Forest Service was charged to protect the habitat, the land, and the local economy, our local industries of timber and ranching from outside, unfair interests," he pauses and then restates, quite firmly, this last phrase. **"To protect our local industries of timber and ranching from outside, unfair interests."**

His statement confuses me—elk? outside interests?—until a woman in the audience rises to explain. Womanlike, she tries to defuse the confrontation.

"Our fight is not with the Forest Service," she says. "It's with these ego-environmentalists who want this country returned to wilderness. They're the ones putting pressure on Congress. These people are ridiculous! They're ridiculous! And they're trying to get rid of us. This is a well thought-out plan."

The facilitator intervenes to talk about the need not to "label" people or name-call.

A spokesman from the National Rifle Association picks up the woman's point and enlarges on it. "Gentlemen," he begins, "I want to warn you about something. There is an unseen presence in this room. There is a third force here today, and I know of what I speak, for we in the National Rifle Association have been driven to our knees by the environmentalists. Gentlemen, these people command millions and millions of dollars, of TV and advertising time! They are looking over your shoulder! Gentlemen, the genie is out of the bottle! You can't win an argument on an environmental issue. If it comes down between cows and elk, you are going to lose!"

I look about the room of thirty men and five women, some sitting forward, drinking in these words, others with their arms still crossed, their faces blank. I look at the few "environmentalists" here; I know them by name and would know them anyway by their hairstyles and clothing. I understand why they have not spoken up in this last hour of comment. There is too much passion swirling through this room, too much fear behind these blank faces.

The fear, and the discussion this morning, goes beyond the problem of elk. There are many people in this country, some associated with the far-left environmental group Earthfirst! and some not, who don't want cows grazing on the public lands. There are slogans in the political wind like "Cattle free by '93" or the more silly "No more moo by '92." Every rancher here can quote these slogans, and nearly every one has cattle on the Gila National Forest or the Gila Wilderness or the nearby Aldo Leopold Wilderness. Although these ranchers refuse to admit it, their real fight is not with Earthfirst!ers but with the heartless and compelling logic of numbers.

The West produces 20 percent of the country's beef. Less than 5 percent of the nation's cattle graze on the public lands. (Sheep graze too, but most of the forage is consumed by cows.) Only 31,000 ranchers or corporations lease grazing permits from the federal government, but they proceed to crop 268 million acres: 89 percent of our Bureau of Land Management land and 69 percent of national forest. The majority of wildlife refuges, many wilderness areas, and some national parks and monuments are also grazed.

The health of these lands is unclear. In 1988, the United States General Accounting Office surveyed range managers who estimated, conservatively, that 27 percent of grazing allotments are threatened with damage or actually declining "because authorized livestock grazing levels were higher than the land could support." The managers also felt that conditions and trends were simply unknown for another quarter of the public lands. In 1986 the BLM issued its report that 59 percent of its land was in fair or poor condition, the lower two of four categories. The Forest Service surveyed fifty million acres and decided that 54 percent of its land showed 0–50 percent of its potential natural community—in other words, of the native plants and animals it once supported. The numbers are worse depending on who is computing them. They are far worse when one just considers riparian or streamside areas. They are usually worse in the Southwest. In 1989 the National Wildlife Federation considered 72 percent of New Mexico's public land to be ecologically unsatisfactory.

Ironically, the repeated statement that the American range is in its best condition ever in this century is probably true, given the extreme destruction of the nineteenth century on through World War I and the 1930s. The truth is that most of the West is simply too dry for sustained, heavy grazing—even the buffalo knew that and stayed out of places like Arizona. The best lands for ranching were snapped up by private citizens. What remained—the public land—is the most rugged, the most fragile, and the least suited for cattle. Still, these lands are our watersheds. They are our recreation areas. They are a refuge for wildlife and a gift to our grandchildren. Should we be risking them for beef grown more easily and at less cost in Missouri?

It's no wonder that public lands ranchers feel threatened! Organizations like the Cattlemen's Association, uniting both public and private lands ranchers, were once strong and effective lobbyists. Reagan was a part-time rancher, and for eight years men wearing cowboy hats determined land use policy. All this served to hide what is becoming more obvious to politicians and resource managers. Public lands ranchers are not only outnumbered. They are outnumbered by men and women equally passionate about the subject of bunchgrass or the placement of water tanks. The Sierra Club has nearly fifteen times as many members as there are public lands grazers. The National Wildlife Federation has a membership of five million.

At this meeting, and across the West, it is not only ranchers who feel threatened. Many of the people here came down from small towns and one-store stops nestled against the shoulder of the Gila National Forest or tucked within its very heart. Recently, Forest Service guidelines that protect the Mexican spotted owl and its associated old growth forest have meant reductions in the local timber for sale. For this, and other reasons, mill operations are cutting back.

"Our timber industry is about lost," says the man who will later pound the table. "And just about everyone in our county uses public lands or depends on their revenue. We don't have enough private property for a tax base to support our schools and our county government. We just passed a school bond bill. Who's going to pay for that, for our kids' education? "

"The environmental movement has gone beyond Homo-sapiens," another rancher agrees. "It's human beings damned and be damned! If we don't do something about it, we're going to lose our rural communities. We're just going to disappear."

"You're going to lose anyway," intones the man from the National Rifle Association. "The environmentalists will get you!"

"Well," drawls a voice from the far back of the room. "They'll have spur marks on them if they try."

A number of people smile. I am not sure how I feel. In part, I feel bullied. I resent all this hard masculine anger. I resent the ease of these violent metaphors. At the same time, I like ranchers and want them to like me. The analysis of this goes beyond the romance of films and cigarette commercials. I have watched my son—not my daughter—yearn to be a cowboy ever since he was eleven months old. I have watched him collect a sizeable herd of toy horses. I have made innumerable halters out of yarn and string. As my son grows older, I have had to make rules as to how and when ropes can be swung in the house and which pieces of furniture can double as calves. I have been impressed and appalled by his obsession to dominate his rocking horse. This is, I think, more primal than cultural; this is biology. This is an embrace of power and competence and, yes, joy in the physical world. When I admire this physicality, I am admiring those very ranchers who set their spur marks so firmly on the land.

The facilitator is smiling, perhaps with relief, as he announces a lunch break. The meeting will reconvene in one hour. As I walk out into the windy spring afternoon, dry as the leaves on the dying trees, dry as the yellow hills in this year of drought—we all know that the problem is weather as much as elk—I am struck by how much ranchers and environmentalists have in common. Both believe the other side is powerful, wealthy, ignorant, and ruthless. Both believe the government is their adversary. Both believe they need to educate the public about range management. Both believe they are concerned with the protection of natural resources.

On the sidewalk, next to my parked car, the meeting has spilled out into a voluable group who stand talking among themselves. They look at me warily. Some of them know that my husband is an outfitter in the Gila Wilderness. They all know, by my hair and clothing and because New Mexico is that small a state, that I am not a rancher. A woman from the Mimbres Valley finally greets me: "Well, Sharman, are you for us or against us?"

In half an hour I have driven thirty miles east and am at the place where Highway 90 enters a mountain pass and the Mimbres Valley comes into view. The Black Range, named for its dark fur of trees, defines the horizen with bold calligraphy. Below these mountains, the hills lump and fold like shaggy beasts descending into the valley bottom. Seventy percent of the West is grazed, and in the Mimbres I would guess that number to be more like ninety. If the land is not someone's backyard or garden, then a cow is probably on it. I am so used to this dry and rocky country—I am so used to fence lines grazed brown on one side but still grassy on the other—that like ranchers themselves I hardly see anymore what is healthy and what is not. Now, from the car, I can tell that some of these private pastures have more dirt than forage. The presence of plants like snakeweed, beargrass, and buckhorn cholla also suggest overgrazing, although at this time of year it's easy to blame cattle for what too many clear blue skies have done. Later I will go to the Forest Service and be told that on the nearby public lands there are, indeed, allotments that look pretty bad, that there are, basically, too many cows in the forest.

Here in the Mimbres Valley most of the ranches are what a local economist calls "heartbreak operations." North, near the headwaters of the river, are a few big places like the Ponderosa, which has a lease to run eight hundred cows on the Gila National Forest. At the lower end is the Nan Ranch, with fifteen hundred cows, over one hundred thousand private acres, and a bare sliver of BLM land. Typically, both these large ranches have absentee owners. In the middle of the valley are the small homesteads. A few of these have long, irrigated, emerald fields upon which black Angus and white Charolais look pleasantly pastoral. The majority also have grazing leases on public forest in the Black Range or on the lower BLM land. How many of these ranchers make a living from their cows is hard to say. Often enough, a rancher's wife is a nurse or schoolteacher. The rancher himself may have a part-time job or work as a truck driver at the copper mines.

Socially, the ranching community is going strong. The night lights of the Mimbres Valley Arena Rodeo come on around the Fourth of July and from our house, on many Sundays, we can hear the tinny voice of the announcer. The Cowbelles can boast over fifty members; as a way of promoting beef, these women give chunks of meat to high school home-ec classes and distribute gift certificates to senior citizens. There are, of course, the usual number of feuds between neighbors and within families in which the children must split up a one income ranch. A fair handful of these ranchers are second and third generation; their grandmothers were promoting beef when the Gila National Forest was still a twinkle in some administrator's eye. Ethnically, most of the ranchers are Anglo. (It is Hispanics who keep to the tradition of farming, patterning the valley floor with apple orchards and corn fields.) After living here for ten years, my own contact with ranchers is still friendly and still minimal. The ones I know well tend to be black sheep: Bob Jacobsen practices Ai-kido, Frankie Hudson is both a woman and a vegetarian.

Cows and apples and corn. Twenty years ago, that about summed up the Mimbres Valley. Since then the population has probably quadrupled, with the newcomers a mix of retirees and people like me who work in Silver City or Deming. Most days, when I come home from Silver City, that moment of revelation— through the mountain pass—confirms in me my decision to move here. The pastel colors seem exactly right, the hills in proportion to the lift of Cooke's Peak. Now, in the fallout of this meeting, I see a pall over the land, a division, and a paranoia.

Are you for us or against us?

August is our true spring. The summer afternoon rains have had a chance to green the hills. Penstemon, lupine, and scarlet beards-tongue bloom in the pastures along the road. This morning my husband has coaxed me into riding with him to Bob Jacobsen's ranch, just behind our house and ten miles through pink rock canyon, a jump to the ridge, a gallop over the mesa, then descent again, sliding the slope. I understand that I am nervous riding because I am not yet competent. I am not in control, and I don't know why. As a younger woman, I had my share of physical courage. I felt stronger than the world around me. Now, although I see clearly the power of horsmanship, some layer of fear has grown up over the years. Something undermines me. Still, I want that centaur magic. I want that leap into animalism, and so I keep riding, irregularly, not enough to get better, just enough to hone my fear and desire.

Bob and Norma Jean Jacobsen are new friends. We met them at the local hot springs, where people bathe nude and ranchers don't go. Bob is forty years old and has been cowboying and ranching for over twenty years. For twelve of those years, he was content to just cowboy, riding the ranges of western New Mexico, bunking with the boys, and working his way up to foreman. Eventually he got married and stood at the highest rung of the cowboy's career ladder: he bought himself a ranch.

The economics of this are instructive. What Bob really bought was eighty acres of deeded land, with an attached Forest Service permit to graze 280 cows on sixty sections in the Gila National Forest. One section is 640 acres. This means that the Forest Service felt that five cows could feed themselves per 640 acres of Bob's lease. That amounts to land that is pretty marginal although, as Bob points out, not unusual in the West. Also on Bob's deeded property was a one-room shack that had no electricity, telephone, or running water. For all this, he went into debt for half a million dollars. For the grazing permit alone, he paid to the previous owner $1,000 per animal unit or $280,000. This did not include the cows themselves, which he had to buy.

Each year Bob and Norma also pay a grazing fee to the Forest Service. The fee fluctuates with politics and cattle prices and in 1990 was $1.81 per cow per month. To lease non-irrigated private land would be three or four times more. Some environmentalists object to the low cost of the public lands fee, and out of this comes the phrase "welfare ranching." But Bob points out that the government subsidizes almost every public lands user; each year, for example, the Forest Service operates its recreation program at a loss of millions of dollars. He also refutes the claim that low grazing fees give public lands ranchers a competitive edge. In his mind, the expense of managing cows in rugged terrain and the initial price tag of the grazing permit offset any advantage. In addition, ranchers on public lands bear some costs in maintaining improvements like fences and water tanks.

Like most ranchers here, Bob and Norma Jean run a cow and calf operation, caring for cattle year-round, selling off 90 percent of calves and 10 percent of older cows each fall. The previous owner of their ranch had tried to raise steers which are bought young, fattened, and then sold. This rancher overstocked the range by running a thousand yearlings (considered the equivalent of five hundred mature cows) only six months. When the Jacobsens got here, the land was already overgrazed. A dry winter and spring meant an increase in predator loss, and that first year one bear alone killed twenty calves. Norma spent a lot of time alone with the two kids. The water in the tanks dropped low. The cows grew painfully thin.

In their second year at the ranch, Bob met with the Forest Service and agreed to reduce his herd by forty-five head. The Forest Service, in turn, promised to do a range study in seven years to see if the number of cows could go back up. This agreement was strictly verbal, and Bob made sure that his original allotment of 280 cows was still "on the books." Although the Forest Service doesn't consider a grazing permit to be property, it is treated as such—banks lend money on that 280 number, the value of Bob's deeded land is based on it, and the IRS will tax it as part of his estate. Such "temporary non-use agreements" are not uncommon on the Gila Forest. The forest ranger can also permanently reduce an allotment, but for now this is considered a draconian measure.

To me, to my husband, and probably to Norma Jean, Bob's workday is enviable. He's independent. He's outside. He is connected, in a way that we are not, to the natural world and the passing of seasons.

Spring is the time to ride the high pastures and gather cows, perhaps as many as thirty in one morning. The days are so clear that sometimes he can see all the way to Mexico. As the weeks go by, only the stragglers, the wild ones, are left, hidden in the sculpted rock of back canyons or staring down defiantly from a scrub oak ridge. Pushing his horse through thickets of brush or charging across a mesa, Bob is lucky now to get three or four cows in a full day. When they are finally corralled, the cattle are branded, vaccinated, dehorned, and castrated. Then they're moved to summer pasture, and Bob begins the labor of fixing dams, digging postholes, stringing fences, and repairing windmills. In the fall, he gathers again, sells, and takes the remaining herd to their winter home. Winter is slow. Maybe he'll ride up to break ice in a tank or pack in some salt. In part because his land is so mountainous, Bob does almost all his work on a horse.

Also, instead of a modern squeeze-chute and branding table, he ropes his cows, pinning them to the ground like they do at the rodeo. Like many ranchers, he relishes tradition.

The rewards of this are Zen-like, immediate, limited to the working day. After twelve years of ranching, Bob has managed to upgrade his house to include a living room and flush toilet, but it hasn't been easy. Overall, he guesses that he averages $40,000 a year. This keeps him well in debt, what with his interest payments. What keeps him going are his low costs (horse feed and horse shoes) and a love of the lifestyle.

Recently Bob has been borrowing books from us, subscribing to new magazines, seeking a window on an outside world of backpackers and deep ecologists, a world of five billion people. This is not his first psychic rumbling. A few years ago, he jettisoned the cowboy image. "For a long time, I thought it was the wildest, most wonderful life a person could lead," he once told me. "But a cowboy has to dress a certain way. He has to talk a certain way. He has to think a certain way. It's a dead end. Finally, I didn't want to be that confined. I didn't want to be just what a cowboy is supposed to be."

It was sometime later that Bob went into ungrazed parts of the Gila Wilderness for the first time. He was "bowled over" by its beauty—not, he says, the approved cowboy reaction. The next year he and his family attended a three-day celebration of the 1964 Wilderness Act, sponsored here by the Forest Service. Other local ranchers boycotted the event, and the New Mexico Farm and Livestock Bureau demanded an audit of expenses. These protests were both vehement and deeply rooted. Historically, the rancher's role has been to tame wilderness, not celebrate it.

"Ranchers look at wilderness on the map and see it as another place for cows," Bob says. "I don't always like what we have to do in order to survive. Maybe we see erosion. Maybe we know we should pull out some cattle because it hasn't rained much and the land is suffering. Maybe we read that killing predators isn't good in the long run. But we have to bury those things. We have to repress all that if we want to survive."

Survival. When we reach Bob and Norma's ranch that day, I am relieved that, once again, my horse (who is twenty years old) has not pitched me down a mountain or thrown me into a cactus. We are barely on the ground before Bob tells us that he and Norma Jean have found a buyer for their ranch.

I am amazed. I didn't know they were looking for one.

Inside the house, Bob is a little manic. He is a big man, and I have wondered before if half his charisma didn't come from that, from plain bigness. Now he seems to fill up the living room. I can't help but think of all the bears he has shot. He is much like a bear now, pacing, shambling, cornered.

"We could have gone on," he says. "I think ranching is viable if you're smart and a good manager. But I got tired of all the worrying. Worrying about the weather, worrying about interest rates, worrying about what the government was going to do. I could hardly enjoy it anymore. I couldn't ride up a canyon without counting how many fence posts I might get from the juniper trees. I couldn't enjoy the spring because I knew how damned dry it was. I couldn't enjoy the summer for wondering when it was going to rain or the fall for wondering if it would rain too much and I wouldn't get the cattle in."

Norma Jean is setting out food and drink and tending to her children at the same time. These things, not the ranch, have always been her center of power. Bob turns suddenly and asks the question we have not dared ask him. His voice is a well-mannered Western monotone, still soft, still unwilling to scale new ranges of grief and hope and giddy excitement. He has never gone to college. He knows one thing only and knows it well. "What am I going to do now?" he asks Norma.

A few miles from here lives a woman named Sherri who doesn't much care for Bob. They have never met, but for Sherri, a divorced mother with two sons, it is enough that Bob is a public lands rancher.

When Sherri came to the Mimbres Valley, she too had a dream. With money she saved working as a secretary, she bought five acres of irrigated land, thinking to farm intensively and solar-dry her products. Sherri is a smart woman. But her dream couldn't withstand two dry summers followed by a flood and plague of grasshoppers. Rather soon, she had to get a job in town to support her life in the country. Last year, she let her fields be taken over by Johnson grass. She has begun to brood in her adobe house on the hill, and part of her brooding concerns cows.

Unlike environmentalists who don't live near cows, Sherri's grudge is personal as well as political. She believes that overgrazing in the upstream watershed was in part responsible for the "hundred-year flood" that destroyed her raspberries and swept away my car a few winters ago. She maintains that if it weren't for cows, I would still own that Volkswagen. She believes the reason our friends, Jack and Roberta Greene, sold their land was because, for two years in a row, steers broke in and ravished their garden. It broke her heart to see it, and she is certain that it broke theirs. (Since the entire Mimbres Valley is still open range, there is little any of us can do when cattle come bumbling through our orchards and fields. Legally, it is our job to fence them out, and although damages can be claimed, the channels are tortuous and we have to collect the money ourselves—from the very rancher who couldn't or wouldn't put money into his own fences. At any rate, the value of a garden or a favorite peach tree is not really claimable.)

With a passion that seems disproportionate (unless you, too, work indoors in town all day) Sherri will recount some of the hikes she has taken with her sons. "We were walking up a narrow canyon, up to Cooke's Peak, and these cows are preceding me, dropping shit everywhere, drooling shit, immediate and *fresh*, all the way up. We had to watch where we put our feet every step! Yesterday we went down the East Fork of the Gila River, and there were cows everywhere! This is in the wilderness itself! This is supposed to be pristine!"

Sherri is among those who would like to see ranchers off the public lands. She notes that the current grazing fees, as low as they are, pay only one-third of the cost of the BLM and Forest Service grazing management programs. In 1986, that cost was

$63 million. Sherri, to be sure, is a storehouse of facts and figures. She can tell you how many coyotes, bear, and mountain lions were killed in New Mexico last year by the Department of Agriculture at the request of ranchers. She can tell you at what rate riparian cottonwood habitat is disappearing in Arizona, which bird and animal species are endangered by overgrazing, and the percent of water taken from the Colorado River to grow hay for cattle.

"What about the people themselves?" I ask her. "The men and women who have worked years on a ranch, who love the lifestyle, who know nothing else?"

"What about *me*?" Sherri snaps. "I would love to have an agricultural lifestyle. I'd love to get up at sunrise and work hard in the garden, in the earth all day. But it's not possible. I can't afford it, and no one has offered to subsidize me. I'm a secretary instead, and if I don't want to be a secretary, then I have to find, all on my own, something else to do."

She hears herself and doesn't like it. She is vice-president of the Native Plants Society, she has a degree in botany, she has gone to jail to protest a nuclear power plant. She does not need to base her dislike of public lands ranching on envy.

"We are becoming a desert," Sherri says. "It's been progressive since the cattle came. A third of North America has undergone severe to very severe desertification, and some people think this is what the West *is*, a desert, and it's *not*. Just read about what was here, before the 1880s, and you know: we're choosing this. We'll never see the land the way it once was. We'll never regain what we lost. But we can't afford to lose any more!"

The next day Sherri telephones me. She has been thinking about the rancher's point of view, and now she has a plan. She points out that Silver City could use an adobe industry, that people are looking for adobes and shipping them in from as far away as Albuquerque. She suggests that local ranchers trade in their four-wheel drive pickups to invest in adobe machines. "It's hard work," she enthuses. "It's outside. It's physical. It's what they are used to."

There is a long silence on the phone. I can not imagine the ranchers I know making adobes. I tell her that, realistically, they would rather be on a horse.

"They can ride on the weekend," Sherri says, "like the rest of us."

She is implacable.

John Forgue is different from me or Sherri or Bob Jacobsen in that John's grandfather came here in 1908. Alongside his dad, John began riding up to the Black Range, where his ranch has a national forest lease of seventy sections, before he began first grade. When he finished high school, he stayed right here, working for ranches up and down the valley. When his father died unexpectedly, John took over the family ranch. He runs 237 cows on his leased land (five years ago he took a temporary reduction) and another hundred on his eight sections of private land. He is a third generation rancher who married the daughter of a nearby rancher and who hopes that his only child, a boy, will be a rancher too. Long before I met him, I had heard about John: the best cowboy in the Mimbres Valley, a man admired by other men for his roping, his endurance, his way with horses. John and his wife live in a trailer down five miles of dirt road and beautiful scenery. I do not expect to ever learn that they have just found a buyer.

John's cramped living room is dominated by a mountain lion's skin on the wall and a gleaming wood cabinet full of trophies with brass horses on top. His wife is out catching a straying bull. Sitting on the edge of a fake-leather armchair, John carefully removes his hat. He is willing to talk to me because he thinks that the rancher's side of the story is not being told.

"The legitimate rancher isn't about to abuse the land or overgraze it because that's his livelihood," John explains. "If we abuse the land, what will we have ten years from now? I'm looking down the road here. I'm looking out for the future."

I have heard ranchers say this before, that taking care of the land was "just good business," and like other things I've heard— "If it weren't for ranchers, there wouldn't be wildlife" or "The rancher was the first environmentalist"—it hasn't always rung true. It simply isn't true for many ranches that are absentee owned, bought for the tax write off, bought as a second income, bought as a form of semi-retirement, or bought as a kind of Western playground.

On the table beside me are pictures of the Forgue son. Framed and obviously taken by a professional, they show the boy first as a baby, a toddler, and then a sturdy third-grader with freckles and slicked down hair. When John Forgue says he's working for the future, I believe him. When he says he's not getting rich off his cows, I believe him too. So I ask him why he keeps on ranching. I ask him why he doesn't sell his land to developers, invest the money, and take his wife to Hawaii.

John sits back in his armchair.

"Gosh," he says. "That's a good question."

At first, suspiciously, I can't believe he has not thought of it himself. But his answer has all the pauses and circles of a heartfelt belief never before articulated.

"I can't explain it," he tries. "It's my home, I guess. Even that old Forest Service land, which we don't own, which we only lease, it's home to me. I can go up there and be working cattle, just off out there by myself, and that's where I'm the happiest. That's just what I am."

This is, I suppose, the answer I was fishing for. I know a few other people who are "happiest in nature" but for various reasons none of them followed that happiness. It is not a daily affair. It is not so imbued in their life as to be unnamed, unexamined, or uncorrupted.

For various reasons, I am personally glad that John is at home in the Black Range. It gives me hope.

John and I are strangers and of different gender, and having shared a moment of intimacy, we both react against it. For a while, we talk about easier things, about changes in the valley and how it saddens him to see more lights at night, more trash on the forest from overnight campers, more four-wheelers tearing up the grass. He is polite: "I know it's progress. You all live in one of those subdivisions, don't you? But I hate to see the river being cut up like it is." We talk about beef prices, which are good now, $1.20 per pound for a four-hundred-pound calf. John is quick to say that as the supply builds up, the prices will go down again. His family survives by putting money aside for leaner years. We talk about the weather—a ritual we missed before—until finally I return to the disagreeable subject I have come to talk about.

And John says that, no, he does not think the public lands are in bad shape or that we need less grazing or more wilderness. He thinks the land needs to be productive. This is his main point: you can't eat scenery. He believes that if "we take more and more land out of production the American people will ultimately suffer. We've got to have food. We've got to have our timber and our ranching. We've got to have houses and paper to write on. I'm afraid we'll wake up some day and not have these things and there won't be anyone around who still knows how to do it."

John also thinks that as the government starts interfering more with public and private lands, "us and Russia are kind of reversing roles." He's heard about how environmentalists sabotage ranchers. He has read that in northern New Mexico they poison salt blocks. He thinks these people should be caught and prosecuted. He thinks his own land, public and private, is pretty healthy. He thinks that ranching is a full time job and says that a rancher has to get out and keep the cows scattered, keep them away from streams, keep them moving. He comes back, as ranchers do now, to fear.

"All they have to do is raise those grazing fees," he says. "People like me, the family ranch, the small ranch, we'd be out of business."

John Forgue is ready to listen as well as talk. "We can't deal with those radical groups like Earthfirst! That 'Cattle-free by '93' stuff. But people in the Sierra Club or the Audubon Society, they're the type we could work with and should work with. That's what it's going to come down to. Ranchers and non-ranchers. We have to sit down and work out our differences."

I am reminded of another conversation with another rancher. "It's changing, changing every day," he told me, and I could see him seeing it. "That train is coming."

I remember talking to a young Forest Service official, off the record, after the elk and livestock meeting. "These ranchers will have to change the way they do business." His voice, too, was serene and implacable. "They'll have to reduce and manage more. Whether they stay is up to them."

An hour later, when I leave the Forgue place, I shut their gate tight, in the momentary conviction that there is a place for their son on our public lands. In the same way that we need Mexican spotted owls, we need ranchers like John Forgue. We need a width and breadth of human experience.

When I get home, my husband tells me that a herd of elk are jumping fences to eat alfalfa on a neighbor's irrigated field—just a mile from our own. We have never heard of elk coming down so low. I have never heard of an elk in this valley.

In the coming week, the Arizona Cattle Growers' Association will demand that over 60 percent of Arizona's twenty thousand elk be reduced and that the government pay damages to public lands ranchers. This is hardly the spirit of compromise, in a state where ranchers number less than four thousand (about fifteen hundred on public lands) out of over three million people. In

New Mexico, too, some ranchers are claiming that their grazing rights have, ipso facto, become property rights which the government is obliged to protect against the encroachment of wildlife. Through usage and tradition, they say, the public land is now theirs.

When I asked John Forgue why he didn't go to the elk and livestock meeting, he told me that he prefers to stay at home and mind his own business. "But maybe I'm at fault," he mused, "for not getting out there more to give my views. Maybe the time is past for staying at home."

Maybe he's right, I think.

Changing, changing every day. And not all the changes are for the worst. I like the wildness implied in having elk behind my hill.

I also like living in a community of ranchers.

I am not sure they will both be here in twenty years time.

BIOSPHERE II

Driving four hours from Silver City, New Mexico to the Biosphere II project in Tucson, Arizona, my husband and I began to talk about Montana. This was our first trip, alone and together, since the birth of our son two years ago. Leaving our children at daycare, we set out feeling shamelessly gay, eating a breakfast of Snappy Mart burritos and watching the Burro Hills untangle in the window. In half an hour, we had descended two thousand feet and could see the high plain of the Chihuahuan Desert.

Montana is where we met and fell in love, and after ten years what we carried away from there still resonates, niggles, annoys, and persuades. Montana is a glamorous state which has received, perhaps, more than its share of good press. There are reasons for this. Writers are attracted to places of power, and Montana is powerful. Physically, it is grand. Impossibly high mountains rear on the horizen and often enough there is nothing around—no city, motel, or convenience store—to distract you from this sight. The scene is action stopped. The mountain rears, and you are on the ground. Wildlife still abounds in Montana, and it is still frightening. Grizzly bears eat people almost every summer, and for every summer I was there it was someone I vaguely knew. In winter, snow falls with gusty celebration, and on very cold days, as I jogged the outskirts of Missoula, I imagined falling and twisting my ankle. I imagined freezing to death. Although the nearness of death is a state attraction, there are, as well, softer beauties. There are yellow fritillaries that open in green meadows and, for someone from the Southwest, there is an abundance of flowing water: eddies, gushes, creeks, streams, rivers that import wildness into the heart of town. Montana is beautiful and, to their credit, the people there know and cherish that.

Sometimes the way Montanans cherish things can get a little strange, and my husband and I talked about that too. In our time, at least, there was a righteous xenophobia and a tribal sense that we are the People, and you are not. There was, from this woman's point of view, a masculinization that had grown hard and brittle, like an insect's shell. Although these things were, in part, why I left, the romance of Montana continues to compel me, even as I distrust it.

"I have Montana voices," I told my husband as we skewered onto the interstate, past the sad town of Lordsburg with its abandoned motels—someone's last hope, someone's failed dream. "And every once in a while, I ask them for approval. Or I know that they disapprove. Am I genuine enough? I ask them. Am I real?"

Well, we all have voices. Usually they are a mixed bag: shrill, numinous, or both at the same time. I have another one from my

Kansas grandmother and yet another from a sixth grade science teacher. At its best, it is the Montana voice that talks to me of my connection to the earth. This was the voice that pushed and followed my husband and me to southwestern New Mexico, where within three months of our arrival we bought twelve acres of grama grass, yucca, and scrub oak. For more than we could afford, we bought on the Mimbres River, thirty miles from town, for the land had to be irrigated. We had to have water, a garden, a farm. There was no question about that. When we began to build our house, we had to do that ourselves. We had to make each adobe brick. We had to have chickens and goats. We had to design a privy that would compost our wastes and return them in usable form. We had to have a homebirth for our first child. Each year, whether he went hunting or not, my husband had to have a deer license. Each year, we had to plant a new bed of perennials.

These were unconscious decisions. These were shoulds that hardly took into account our own natures or the practicality of earning a living and raising children. Unknowingly we were following voices. We were struggling to become real.

Our appointment at Biosphere II was for 1:00 P.M. and so we took the fast route, becoming part of the herd on Interstate 10, reveling, even on that road, at the beauty of the landscape: vistas of yellow grass that turn to the lavendar of distant mountains, hills like the bare bones of a cow, playas twinkling in and out of existence.

On my lap, I held a folder of press releases and magazine clippings. Although its completion date was over a year away, Biosphere II had already gotten considerable attention. Meant to be a prototype for space colonies, this for-profit, privately funded project aims to duplicate the cycles of Earth in a self-contained environment. Eighty-five feet high, glittering with glass, the arched space-frame structure and its stainless steel floor now covers some three acres. As a final step, using newly developed sealants and a double door airlock, the entire building is corked airtight so that nothing but information—electronically conducted—and solar energy can enter.

For the inside of this miniature world, the designers really got ambitious. There are five biological communities: a rain forest, savannah, salt water marsh, ocean, and desert. There is also a one-half acre organic farm and a six-story white-domed apartment building with library, laboratory, offices, and exercise room. Nearly four thousand plant and animal species inhabit Biosphere II with five thousand sensors to monitor them. Water and air circulate naturally and mechanically. Rain falls on the rain forest, gathers into a stream, tumbles down a waterfall, flows across the savannah, spreads over a marsh, and sinks into the thirty-five foot deep ocean—where the water evaporates, rises to cooling condensers, and falls again as rain. The "trade winds" are driven from the desert to the forest by the heat of the sun and blown back to the desert by large fans. There are elaborate systems of purification and huge attached "lungs" that can expand and contract with shifts of atmospheric pressure. In December of 1990, eight carefully selected scientists sealed themselves into Biosphere II to live, independent of outside resources, for two years.

Like a lot of people, I am entranced with the idea and imagine myself one of those carefully selected eight. Like a lot of people, I begin to think in Biblical terms: Genesis, Eden, Noah's Ark. In this case, Eden has another and more social resonance, for in many ways life in Biosphere II will resemble—if all goes as planned—the communal dreams of the sixties. Each morning, the Biospherians wake to a very short commute and a full day of working together. About four hours must be spent on maintenance, with half that time in the "intensive agriculture area." Here, the asparagus needs picking. The pygmy goats must be fed. And, as the chicken population expands, someone has to kill and pluck that young rooster for dinner. Other maintenance chores include fixing leaky pipes and attending to the solar-powered motor with the funny noise. With no electrician or plumber to call in, hands get dirty and thumbs hammered. Economically, it is two years in a consumer vacuum: watching the mangos ripen and rejoicing when the coffee tree bears its single crop.

Once the needs of survival are met, the scientists can turn to individual research. One of the Biospherians is twenty-six-year-old Taber MacCallum, an eclectic youth from Albuquerque who never, actually, got a college degree. MacCallum is now in charge of analyzing air and water quality in Biosphere II, as well as being the assistant medical officer. Other members of the crew have their own specialties. Abigail Alling is a marine biologist; Linda Leigh studies desert plants.

For relaxation, the Biospherians read books, watch movies, swim in the ocean, or stroll through the "wilderness biomes." Like the rest of us, they may get fed up at times and be tempted to leave their unique fishbowl. Like most of us, they'll be stopped by cultural and legal expectations. Although their personal and sexual life is considered private, they are, in fact, public figures. Already the project is preparing a gift shop and future tours of the site. One consultant told me he expects 10,000 people a year to visit Biosphere II.

What if one of the Biospherians gets pregnant? I wonder.

Then, of course, in a medical emergency, the airlock will unlock and the pressure doors open.

At the time of our visit, however, all this was in the future. The project was still conducting rehearsals in its Biosphere II Test Module, and my husband and I were driving to Tucson because at 2:00 P.M. Abigail Alling was going to enter the airtight module and live for five days on home grown papaya and tilapia fish. In a space about as big as my living room, the carbon dioxide she exhaled would be taken up by surrounding plants and transformed into oxygen while her wastes were detoxified and recycled to irrigate her garden of food. In short, this was a mini Biosphere II just as Biosphere II is a mini Earth. (Coyly, the directors of Biosphere II refer to Earth as Biosphere I.) The whole affair was also an elaborate press conference to which my husband and I were invited only after many phone calls and a letter from the children's science magazine for whom we freelance. As journalists from the small town of Silver City, we were, I think, viewed with suspicion. Indeed, we viewed ourselves that way.

At the moment, I was simply happy to be on the road. I was happy to be in the Sonoran Desert, the landscape of my childhood, and an interior landscape that I carry with me like a charm or rarely used pocket mirror. Too quickly we passed through the true arboreal desert with its jumble of cactus and narrow-leafed trees. Then, spinning on the freeway, we entered into Tucson's strange mix of saguaro, oleander, pampas grass, and California poppy. This too was familiar to me. I knew these orange groves bordered by cholla. I knew the look of a Sunbelt strip: fast food, chrome, glitter, asphalt, punctuated by a dirt lot with blooming creosote.

By the time we took the wrong turn, drove through town, and headed north to Oracle Junction and the Biosphere II site, we were running late. A sign on the highway directed us to a stretch of dirt road, a massive iron grill gate, and a forbidding adobe guardhouse. A woman with a clipboard stood out front and bent interrogatively close as each car drove up. We straightened nervously in our seats, but there we were, on the official press list, given official passes, and sent on our way.

This was fun. My husband and I felt in disguise. As we pulled into the parking lot, reporters and TV crews streamed around us, jostling out of expensive-looking cars. An unshaven man hoisted a heavy camera, trailed wires, and scampered past like Carroll's rabbit. My husband and I smiled at each other. For the last four hours we had not argued once but had talked instead about our lives and our dreams. We felt, pleasantly, like students again, young and in love, fresh from Montana.

An asphalt walk wound up to the conference room where Kathleen Dyhr, the director of information systems, was giving a hurried talk. Afterwards, we all wound back down to the test module, which stood on its cement pad like a spaceship pagoda.

At that time, the grounds of Biosphere II already included a number of futuristic buildings, arched and angular, painted in glowing white or shining with glass. Although the mesquite and cholla around me looked diseased, elsewhere there were fine views of healthy desert country and the twenty-five hundred acre ranch that surrounds Biosphere II. I could even see cattle grazing picturesquely.

Against this backdrop, the people who work here had been dressed for effect and wore cardinal red jumpsuits with white and green Bio II logos on the chest. The uniforms seemed a little comical, and I thought of cocktail waitresses forced to don tutus and fishnet stockings. Still, the bright red made the staff stand out, and they all seemed happy. Near the test module was a long table with iced punch, exotic fruits, and a four-foot-long Biosphere II made of white cake and coconut frosting. Speeches were given while the photographers elbowed for room. The TV crews frowned and barked at each other. The writers tended to wander, absorbing ambiance and eating cake.

"Let the experimenter enter the experiment!" Abigail Alling said gayly. After she did, we milled about and watched her wave to us from inside the glass and steel module. Then we were prodded back to the conference room.

In the next few hours, I found Biosphere II to be both more and less than it had seemed to be on paper.

As we toured the greenhouses that grew the plants for the five biomes, I was reminded that the project itself could be called nothing more than a glorified greenhouse. Despite the allusions I had read, this was artifice, not Creation. The agriculture area, in particular, made me uneasy: the vegetables were too rigorously weeded, too neatly and symmetrically placed in their beds. Heads of lettuce, sheathed in plastic, protruded from a wall in an experiment I could not decipher. Tilapia fish swam in prosaic drums where the ammonia they excreted was routed by pipes to be converted to nitrates. Agriculturally speaking, it was a connection to process, not to land. Anarchy had been banished. Efficiency was all.

At the same time, the people involved in Biosphere II became more comfortably real as the day wore on. Much of what they said was familiar, for I had heard versions of it in other interviews. Clearly, these men and women had had experience with the press. Yet they were not jaded.

"It's obvious in Biosphere II," said Mark Nelson, chairman of the London Institute of Ecotechnics and a major consultant for the project, "that the same techniques we need to extend man into space are precisely the tools we need to sustain man on earth! To create Biosphere II, we have to understand the world of life and the world of technology and have them work together. Ecologists here have to talk to engineers. They have to learn each other's language!"

Mark was youthful and well-groomed and effusive. On the basis of a first impression, he struck me as an idealist. I asked him what in concrete terms we could expect to gain from Biosphere II.

"You don't throw anything away in this biosphere," he said. "And if you put a chemical somewhere, it'll soon end up in your glass of water. I think we'll learn about how to deal with the environment, how to live on this planet, and how to take our biosphere with us and live off the planet!"

I would discover that getting man off the planet was one of Mark's more eloquent themes. It was not mine, and the question I asked him became the one I focused on.

Carl Hodges, head of the University of Arizona's Environmental Research Lab and another prestigious consultant, answered it with a rat-a-tat list. Dr. Hodges is an older, avuncular kind of man who helped design the Land Pavilion at Disney's Epcot Center in Florida and who projects a sly, jolly, down-to-earth sense of humor. For the moment he seemed tired and bored with repeating himself. In the last hour, I had seen him talk obediently to four different journalists.

"What will we gain? Ways to clean air. Ways to recycle nutrients. Ways to recycle waste. Ways to produce food intensively and without pesticides or other chemicals. Ways to seal up buildings and manage them more effectively."

"Ways to clean air?" I asked, in part to slow him down so that I could scribble out the rest.

"In Biosphere II," he answered, "the air will be forced through soil beds full of microbes that oxidize the toxic gases that tend to accumulate. In two years, I expect us to put a version of such soil beds, a consumer soil bed reactor, on the market for homes and offices. Eventually we should be able to adapt these for cities. In effect, we could be putting our pollution into the dirt to be cleaned rather than into the air to get it dirty."

This was a good quote which I had heard him say before. I imagined huge, boxlike, soil bed reactors against the skyline.

"Why do you think ordinary people, people on the street, get excited about Biosphere II?" I asked.

This may have been a new question, for he roused noticeably. "It is encoded somewhere in us that plants are valuable." He cupped his hands as though enclosing a seed. "In this system, we see very clearly that we are sustained by plants. They take in carbon dioxide and give out oxygen. When people realize that the other half of their lung is that tree over there, they get excited. Their world is enlarged."

Earlier, addressing a roomful of people, Carl Hodges had reminded us of the days when men and women first saw Earth from the vantage of space. From these famous pictures came the ideas of lifeboat Earth, spaceship Earth, Earth as a whole, Earth as a fragile green and blue ball. Carl Hodges believes that Biosphere II could equally shift our consciousness. He believes that the project is historic, revolutionary, and personally wonderful.

His enthusiasm was echoed by other staff members.

To Robert Hahn, director of product development, fell the task of ushering my husband, myself, and three other writers on a larger tour of the grounds. By now it was past the time when most people go home from work, and I suspected that Robert had had a long day. Still, he was a gracious host. Unlike Carl Hodges and Mark Nelson—obvious bigwigs—Robert wore the red uniform and tasteful logo. His job title emphasized the fact that this thirty-seven million dollar project expects to make money. He told us that already there were spinoffs in sealant research and environmental cleanup systems. Ultimately, of course, the main product of Biosphere II will be the ability to create more biospheres. Soon, Robert theorized, a city like Chicago would have a rain forest biosphere much as it has a zoo and art museum. Biospheres can also be used as scientific laboratories: introduce an exotic species into a mini desert and see what happens or, on a more global scale, pump in carbon dioxide and observe the greenhouse effect—then lower the shades and create a nuclear winter.

Up to this point, we had a modest vision: a nice biosphere for the school children to visit or for a university to spend money on. But there was also the grand plan of biospheres underwater, biospheres on the moon, biospheres on Mars, and biospheres drifting in the vacuum of outer space. The director of product development gestured at the horizon for, like Mark Nelson, his thoughts reach out to the sky—limited in Biosphere II, but the metaphor still works.

As we made our way past the tissue culture lab to the insectary, I heard another group leader expound with tenderness on the tall, scraggly, and upside-down boojum tree. "Some of the species we are including in the desert are for aesthetic reasons," the ecologist explained. "We want the people who live here to come to the desert for pleasure and beauty. The smell of this lavender here and the comic effect of the boojum. They're important too."

Elsewhere, in the greenhouses we visited, I had heard similar rhapsodies. Now, on the walk, we met one of the architects of Biosphere II. He was tan and faintly exotic, with what appeared to be a diamond twinkling in one ear. I was not surprised when he exclaimed spontaneously that he loved his job. "It's perfect!" he said. "A chance in a lifetime!"

In the insectary, red-clad entomologist Jane Poynter had just finished talking with another tour. As they left, she turned to us, her smile undimmed. Her role was to help populate Biosphere II with detrivores and pollinators or, in popular language, varieties of bees, wasps, mites, cockroaches, spiders, and dragonflies. She seemed particularly fond of termites, who are necessary in the savannah to aerate the soil, break down grasses, and bring up nutrients. "Aesthetically," she pointed out, "they make big mounds!" I asked her if there would be mosquitos. "Not the biting kind," she assured me. "But we do need mosquitos in the salt water marsh. Their larva feed the fish."

From Jane we learned more about the other animals who would live in Biosphere II. Each of the five biomes had its own consultant and each was choosing a different approach.

In the rainforest, species were being considered on individual merit. The rodent *agouti,* who pollinates by burying seeds and forgetting about them, was considered meritorious. More aggressive and socially-oriented monkeys were not. The pygmy deer called *pudus* and *mazamas* fit nicely into this small ecosystem. ("Ideally, we would have pygmy humans," Carl Hodges once said.) Larger predators would upset the balance. In just one example, considerable effort had been expended to find the right hummingbird to pollinate the thousands of jungle flowers that would bloom daily. Happily, a rufous-tailed generalist from Mexico seemed to fit the bill, with a beak neither too curved nor too straight nor too short.

Picking species, one by one, is a kingly and mythic and fun thing to do. But Walter Adey of the Smithsonian Institute was taking another tack for the marsh and ocean. He chose to dig up actual chunks of a Florida swamp and Caribbean coral reef and transfer them whole to Biosphere II. Over a hundred species of flora and fauna can live in a square meter of marsh, and Adey says he would hardly know which ones to omit and which to keep. He was willing to throw out a few dangerous customers such as liver flukes which cause disease. But Adey does not believe in simplifying. He believes in complexity.

As we were about to leave, Robert asked if we would like to see the construction site where Biosphere II was just then being built. It was a long walk uphill, and he used his hand radio to order a van. I could tell that Robert was pleased to be able to do this, pleased with a technology that is the warp of this project just as nature is the weft. Not everyone, of course, is so continually pleased with Biosphere II. At least one scientist has declared it to be ridiculously ambitious. Why, after all, start with five eco-systems? A jungle and a marsh? A desert and an ocean? Another critic calls it an expensive toy. There is something to this, for the project hums with the kind of excitement that children have for battery operated presents and that humans, in general, have for high tech. (Still, to understate the case, for thirty-seven million dollars, Biosphere II seems to be a bargain—far more interesting than most high-budget movies and many defense projects.)

Above the construction site, we looked down over a scene of giant cranes resting from their labor of lifting the huge skeletal pieces of Biosphere II. Nearby were circular cement pads where the "lungs" would be, attached to the sealed building by an underground tunnel. The Arizona sunset was something else I remembered from my childhood, its brush strokes broad and heavy on the pink. By now, most of the other journalists had gone. My husband took some last photographs of glass buildings turning to gold. Then we thanked Robert, drove home, wrote our article, resumed arguing, and resumed our chosen life—the task of fitting edges together. From a distance we kept watch as Biosphere II also continued, shaping and fitting together the pieces of its own curious dream.

Months later, it takes a neighbor to explain to me the significance of that dream to mine. We have hiked to a ridge above my tin-roofed adobe and its accoutrements of building supplies, one broken car, trash, and a swingset. From this ridge, we can see the long corridor of the Mimbres Valley with its orchards and fields. The dry brown hills lift away from the green like slowly flapping wings.

"Isn't that why we all moved out here?" my neighbor comments. "Weren't we all trying to create our own Biosphere II?"

I look down at my twelve acres where we are now hiring someone to help us put in a flush toilet. We have proven ourselves to be mediocre gardeners and lousy composters. We have discovered that we can not seal ourselves off from the rest of the world and do not really want to. All the structures we erect—borders, state lines, fenced in land, adobe walls—can not shelter us from the fact that we live in one biosphere. City or town or country, we are all one people, a large crowd jostling for space.

Still, I do not think that our instincts, here in this valley—or that subtle xenophobia, there in Montana—were completely wrong. Sometimes, in order to talk to the earth, you need to claim a small part of it first. Sometimes, in order to become human, you need a tribe small enough to hold in your mind.

I look down at my home and, in a sweet rush, I think that I will live here forever. I will grow old here and my walks will be rich with memories enmeshed in the soil, in the rocks, in the junipers. I will know the contours of this land like the wrinkles of my skin. I will own it all!

I think this and, at the same time, I prepare myself to leave. The valley will change too much. Or I will. I tell myself, and I believe this too, that the process of connection has already taken place and the roots are growing inward. Something is growing that I can carry with me—away from here if I must.

I think of Biosphere II, further west still, in the heat of my childhood. It is easy enough to call it foolish, contrived, arrogant in its scope. Yet, when I relax and let it blossom, like a tree in a garden ready to bear fruit, it reverts to its original and powerful image: paradise protected.

Human beings in love, at last, with their world.